THE
Love
TREE

ELYSE ABIEL

WESTBOW
PRESS®
A DIVISION OF THOMAS NELSON
& ZONDERVAN

WestBow Press books may be ordered through booksellers or by contacting:

WestBow Press
A Division of Thomas Nelson & Zondervan
1663 Liberty Drive
Bloomington, IN 47403
www.westbowpress.com
844-714-3454

NIV: All Scripture quotations, unless otherwise indicated, are taken from the Holy Bible, New International Version®, NIV®. Copyright ©1973, 1978, 1984, 2011 by Biblica, Inc.™ Used by permission of Zondervan. All rights reserved worldwide. www.zondervan.com The "NIV" and "New International Version" are trademarks registered in the United States Patent and Trademark Office by Biblica, Inc.™

CEB: Scriptures taken from the Common English Bible® (CEB). Copyright © 2012 by Common English Bible and/or its suppliers. All rights reserved.

GNB: Scriptures and additional materials quoted are from the Good News Bible © 1994 published by the Bible Societies/HarperCollins Publishers Ltd UK, Good News Bible© American Bible Society 1966, 1971, 1976, 1992. Used with permission.

NLT: Scripture quotations marked (NLT) are taken from the Holy Bible, New Living Translation, copyright © 1996, 2004, 2007 by Tyndale House Foundation. Used by permission of Tyndale House Publishers, Inc., Carol Stream, Illinois 60188. All rights reserved.

ISBN: 978-1-6642-0377-8 (sc)
ISBN: 978-1-6642-0379-2 (hc)
ISBN: 978-1-6642-0378-5 (e)

Library of Congress Control Number: 2020916777

Print information available on the last page.

WestBow Press rev. date: 03/05/2021

DEDICATION

For all the people of this beautiful, treacherous world.

CONTENTS

CHAPTER 1
Clear Vision

A flash in the dark,
Illumines our fear.
Twenty-Twenty
A lightning year.

Light from above,
A promise in rain.
Hope of new growth,
As love heals our pain.

Twenty-twenty is a good-looking number, so nice and neat. We felt secure as the year began. Couples planning their weddings, happy to have 2020 as the year of their promise. But the round number rolled in the decade with a silent enemy that swept from east to west. Weddings were not as the brides imagined, if they took place at all. Dating couples mingled from a distance, encapsulated in giant bubbles. March Madness was a fight at near empty shelves rather than the swoosh of basketballs.

A worldwide pandemic besieged us, bringing fear and isolation—so many alone, unable to reach out and touch someone. On the front lines, men and women were pushed to their limits. Those who cared for the sick and the dead clothed themselves with courage. Essential workers worked at risk. For others, homes became work hubs and classrooms. Millions of jobs disappeared. So much change. So much pain.

It was a make-or-break year for relationships. Families sheltered together, forced to engage, experienced shock and enlightenment. Problems could no longer be ignored. For some, more time together brought out the best; for others, their relationships fell apart. People cooped up in poverty had overwhelming stress, even food a worry. It became hard to breathe and then mankind's gentle giant George Floyd called out the words. God had made him beautiful, big, and black. At heart he was not one to be afraid of, yet he had lived with fear. The world at a tipping point. Will it be a turning point?

Life can be fragile and unpredictable. In 2020 our world was shaken. Hundreds of thousands died of a virus we couldn't see. Unrest filled our streets as we struggled to see each other in the fight for justice. Our planet raged with fiery, stormy evidence that it is fragile too. The brevity and adversity of life shakes us; as a young women it hit me hard, changing my perspective forever. We can't help but ask questions. Is there purpose beyond our understanding? Is there more? Now, many years later, I see life as our own personal journey of trial, adventure, province, and growth on a road made to take us home. And so, I write to the world with a wish and a dream—let's seek to find true love.

There was a vision given to us long ago, at the beginning of the age— John's vision. Much of it is frightening, yet it concludes with a symbolic vision of great hope. John sees a new city:

> Then the angel showed me the river of the water of life, as clear as crystal, flowing from the throne of God and of the Lamb down the middle of the great street of the city. On each side of the river stood the tree of life, bearing twelve crops of fruit, yielding its fruit every month. And the leaves of the tree are for the healing of the nations. No longer will there be any curse. (Revelation 22:1–3a)

In this radiant new city, the light shines from God. People from every nation on earth reside in this diverse and beautiful city, each a valued member of one happy family, wanting to serve God and each other forevermore. Love is in the air, and we breathe it freely.

I've imagined that new day, after the storms rage. A new morning rising, following the days when we were not sure the earth would survive. At daybreak, light slowly glimmers above the dark edge of the horizon. The magical glow gradually becomes more vivid. Our eyes behold a rainbow of glowing hues, deep and clear, as though looking through stained glass. Gardens of emerald greens and jewels of radiant color fill our vision—the earth anew. Light filters through the huge healing leaves and dabbles upon the sparkling springs. The tree of life gives shelter to a living family tree, a beautiful tree from every nation and tribe known to earth.

Long ago, under the great trees of shelter, the oaks of Abraham, the plan began to unfold. God would intervene, and an unlikely child would be born. A family tree would take root. Ultimately, each would do what was right and was just. It was the greatest of battles. Many laughed, just as beautiful Sarah did on that day long ago, under the great trees. Few knew the secret to love and justice, and even of those who were told, few believed. Each needed to experience the truth, as they trusted through hardship. Through the struggle, they found rest.

This colorful family tree grew from a root vine—not just any vine, but the invincible vine that had gone through the roughest of weather, even dying, we thought, until rising again to life. The branches of the new tree sprouted slowly at first, but they blossomed as the gardener tenderly cared for them. He cut off the dead and pruned the living, until each branch sprouted others, and so on, and so on; full of life, the tree grew. Each branch received through another, all remaining steadfast to the vine of truth. Wind and storms and evil raged fiercely at times, but the hardships only made the tree grow stronger. You see, this tree shares roots with the eternal tree of life—the oldest tree in the garden, the one that will never die.

The tree of the knowledge of good and evil was thought to have the finest fruit in the garden, juicy, delicious, and very tempting. But the new tree, under the ancient tree-of-life's canopy, now has the most beautiful fruit, far beyond compare. And unique, because this tree grows an amazing variety of fruit, though it is but one tree, connected at the root. At the heart of each fruit is the common seed of true love. This beautiful, vibrant new tree stands strong—God's family tree, the Love Tree.

The security of unconditional love in a beautiful home of healing, this is the hope of everlasting life. The lingering pandemic and outcry for justice wake us from our everyday routines and assumptions. By nature, it's a time of reflection. Is there hope for a world where we are free from evil? Is there life beyond death?

Twenty-twenty is perfect vision, but we could not see what was coming. Why would a loving God allow such hardship and tragedy? Many of our loved ones are gone. Many are living in fear. Is God real? Is he present? Disillusionment brings rise to our questions and doubts. Perhaps God is no more than a fable. Yet the wise know that he is alive and active. Fables and fairy tales have their purpose, but the true Book tells the epic story of God's love for mankind. It assures us that there is a plan. God's story has had a profound effect on my story. In this book I will share a few snapshots of both, flashes of the proof of love.

A storm moves like the wind throughout the world, but the skies will clear. Everything will look brighter, at least for a while. As impurities are washed away, we can see clear water and heavenly wonders. We can see the stars. Look … and see. May God give our world clear vision.

> The voice of the Lord strikes with flashes of lightening. (Psalms 29:7)

> Those who are wise will shine like the brightness of the heavens, and those who lead many to righteousness, like the stars for ever and ever. (Daniel 12:3)

> Blessed is the one who trusts in the Lord,
>   whose confidence is in him.
> They will be like a tree planted by the water
>   that sends out its roots by the stream.
> It does not fear when heat comes;
>   its leaves are always green.
> It has no worries in a year of drought
>   and never fails to bear fruit. (Jeremiah 17:7–8)

"What is the price of five sparrows—two copper coins? Yet God does not forget a single one of them. And the very hairs on your head are all numbered. So, don't be afraid; you are more valuable to God than a whole flock of sparrows." (Luke 12:6–7 NLT)

CHAPTER 2

Nevertheless Hope

Land of hope, don't crush my soul.
Life is hard; I've lost control.

When hope grows dim for love and home,
The songbird calls—you're not alone.

"I have told you these things, so that in me you may have
peace. In this world you will have trouble. But take heart!
I have overcome the world."

—John 16:33

We grow up, hopeful boys and girls, with all kinds of dreams. Dreams
to build things, to find love, to have children, to sing and dance, to be
famous, and to save the world! Somewhere along the line, our hopes are
dashed, often far too early. We realize nothing is as easy as we thought. We
become aware that a lot of bad stuff happens, and some of it is happening
to us. Some of it we are causing! The rose-colored perspective we have about
love and reaching our dreams warps into reality. Experience teaches us that
life is hard, and so is love.

One early winter day, an idealistic young man spotted a truck full of
Christmas trees. The fresh-cut trees looked green and hopeful—a truck
full of joy. That's when a boy from the city decided to become a farmer.
He went off to college and got married. After serving in Japan, post–World

War II, to put the draft behind him, my father and mother bought a small dairy farm. Mom had worked as a phone operator and shared a room with her sister in order to save their pennies while Dad was away. They had no experience farming, but Dad had a degree from agricultural school and a full-time job to pay the bills. They did the best they could with little help. For a short time, we had two foster boys—troubled boys, who did not stay as long as my parents hoped. Their own dreams had been shattered at a young age, or they would not have come to stay with us at all.

Dad got up very early each day, milked the cows, commuted to work in the city, worked all day, traveled home, and milked the cows again. On the weekends, my parents worked on getting water and necessities into the old farmhouse, besides growing grain and hay for the cows and food for us. I was the first of three girls, one child lost, whom my parents believed to be a boy. In the following years, Mom also cared for her mom and sister; Grandma stayed with us at the farmhouse for a time. Both died of ALS.

A full-time job for Dad, part-time for Mom, cows that needed to be milked morning and night, keeping the old farm from falling down around us, harvesting crops, and caring for the people they loved, seeing them suffer, all seems crazy difficult to me! Years later, their treasured historic barn burned down as well.

Life was undeniably hard for my parents, but *they* would say life was good to them. They remembered holidays together, fresh-cut trees, and the children searching for candy treasure on the big front lawn. They could picture their children's delight, feeding a bottle to the calves that were brought into the house to keep warm. There were the smiles of shut-ins gathered for my mom's garden party, weekends with family and friends, and a wedding under the big maple tree.

They remembered the crises averted, such as when their friends and family came together to help them build a new bridge and when they found their two-year-old alive. The farm's half-mile driveway had a high bridge that crossed a major creek. After collecting the milk one day, the milk-truck had broken through. Thankfully, the driver had made it out to come knocking at the door. The truck needed to be pulled off the ledge, and the milk cans had fallen into the creek. As estimates to hire the bridge rebuild came in, my parents realized it would cost more than the mortgage they had taken out to buy the farm. My father later joked that he was one of the few who could rightfully cry over spilt milk.

Before the bridge was rebuilt, my father carried each heavy ten-gallon can of milk across the creek on a plank—a daunting task. One afternoon when my mom came to get me up from my nap, I was missing. Panicked, they looked everywhere! Unforeseen, I had climbed from my crib—a two-year-old with a plan to go berry picking. Basket in hand, I toddled down the hill and across the wooden plank, about twenty feet above a fast-flowing creek, to pick blackberries. My frantic parents later found me up the next hill, with a purple smile! I wonder, if perhaps, an angel was watching over me as I toddled across that plank. Is there something beyond what we see, the way it's pictured in the old storybook illustrations?

My parents were always thankful and looked at the blessings, despite the toll that hardship and loss took on their lives. But let's face it, many of life's stories are without happy endings. Life has its pain, along with its stories of hope and joy. Tragedies, like minefields, interrupt the lives of the living. Disappointments are inevitable. Hardship and sickness cannot be escaped. We all have questions that cry out for answers. My own life story has its share of tragedy, heartache, and unfulfilled dreams. But oh, how I have hope—real, deep-down, honest-to-goodness, well-founded hope! That's what I want to share, flashes of the proof of love.

Late afternoon light flowed through the window; something flickered, and I smiled—a hummingbird at sunset. The speedy, whimsical little bird hovered as if to say hello, its iridescent feathers silhouetted against the sky painted pink and orange above the Pacific. Then it began to dance, flitting back and forth in rhythm, its slender beak moving as if conducting an angelic orchestra.

Nature calls to us. From star-filled galaxies to the colorful aquatic communities of the coral reefs, the natural world has complexity and splendor beyond our wildest imaginings. Consider the peacock—quite an extraordinary bird! Did the peacock originate from a random process? Or did someone imagine beforehand his ornate feathers, topped with the colorful green and blue medallion design that fans out behind him as he struts? The detail and beauty of our natural world give us a measure of evidence of the hope of God. He demonstrates his majesty and power, yet he calls to us individually with surprises in nature, such as my encounter with the magical little hummingbird.

There is no denying that our world is amazingly creative and complex, with dynamic change, remarkable energy and life, even beyond that which we can see. Nature is so intricate and interactive that it is truly beyond our total comprehension. We are delighted and humbled by its beauty and power, experiencing the mixed emotions of wonder, fear, and hope. As the world changes around us, fires and storms raging more and more often, we may be unexpectedly caught—*will I make it through the storm to take my next breath?* And as the storm subsides, overwhelming emotion and relief. The light and color of the sky touch our souls with amazing beauty. We realize we are ultimately not in control—a scary thought. But also comfort and gratitude. I'm alive!

Life is precious, yet there is not always a breath of relief or reprieve. Thousands die in natural disasters each year. Even as I finish writing, we are facing a worldwide pandemic, and hundreds of thousands are dying. Uncertainty looms. Many are anxious and afraid. We have questions. Is God present? Is it true that God is both good and great—both loving and in control? Let's face it, lots of bad stuff happens. Can we believe there is an overriding plan for good that cannot be thwarted? We ask, because that is the clear message of the Bible—God is all-powerful and altogether good, but he also allows nature to take its course and all people to make their own decisions within the life they are given. He allows evil influences to be active in our world as well. Not to say that he never intervenes. Stories of his intervention are common. Nevertheless, everyone faces hardship and evil. Mankind's age-old question remains, "If he really loves us, why would he allow so much suffering?"

God tells us we are his cherished ones, created in his own image (Genesis 1:27). He made each of us unique, creating a world of diversity to reflect an image of himself. If it is true that God exists and created each of us, does he also have a purpose for each of us? The overriding message of the Bible is God's love for us. Can we count on his love in this crazy world? Is it possible his purpose centers around love? The Bible tells us that God is a loving Father, who desires to teach us to love others. If that is true, do our experiences in a world of natural and spiritual forces, both good and bad, prepare us for our future? Will we discover just how dynamic and invincible the power of true love is?

Our lives are full of ups and downs, joy and disillusionment, but if we hang on to hope, we will not be disappointed.

> We rejoice in the hope of the glory of God. Not only so, but we also rejoice in our suffering, because we know that suffering produces perseverance; perseverance, character; and character, hope. *And hope does not disappoint us,* because God has poured out his love into our hearts by the Holy Spirit, whom he has given us. (Romans 5:2–5 NIV1984, italics added)

God is telling us that our character, if rooted in the love of God and developed by life's trials, will be made ready for a hopeful future. He promises we will not be disappointed in the final results. Despite life's hardships, there is a God who sees us and who loves us.

Becoming a truthful and loving person is a process that takes time, and as we learn to love from God himself, our lives become a reflection of the glory of God. A mother with hungry children can look into the eyes of a humanitarian and see hope and life. A young man, struggling to provide for his family, feels the hand of God on him when someone provides him with a job that does not compromise what is right and also pays the bills. A little child feels God's love when a tired parent, at the end of their rope, looks at them and says, "I love you."

To have a life of satisfaction and joy, we need to learn to love and to be loved. It sounds easy, almost natural, but within our relationships, we soon realize it is not easy. It is hard to hear others when no one is listening to us. It is hard to sideline our wants and needs for the sake of someone else. It is hard to relinquish our plan, to commit to someone else's, even if it's a better plan, even if it is God's plan. We are easily distracted or tired, easily hurt, and inwardly focused. As needs are unmet and conflicts arise in our relationships, we become frustrated. Counterfeit comfort pulls us in the wrong direction. Going forward is a struggle.

God cares about our deepest needs and longs to meet us in that struggle. Men and women were created to reflect God's character, yet imparting grace and love to a world in need is not easy. Through the struggle, we meet with God, and he gives us a gift of grace. He teaches us to love ourselves enough to stand up for and do what is right. He helps us learn how to love others, even enough to forgive. Will we pour hate, indifference, impatience, and anger out on our world, or will we hear God's call and learn to love?

Even when we are not sure of God's direction—*Is this God's whisper?*—ask, "Is this action loving and good? Is God asking me to make a change in my life that will improve my relationships?" If so, do it! *Do* the good thing you think you are sensing, whether it is God's idea or yours. Ask him to help you. He is faithful to guide and redirects us as needed, when we desire to do his will. God longs to demonstrate compassion and reveal his reality, in and through our lives. Like the little hummingbird, God has given us the job of passing along his sweet pollen of love. Day by day, he is faithful to show us the way—to help us, correct us, mature us, and most of all, love us. God's love is our hope!

> May the God of hope fill you with all joy and peace as you trust in him, so that you may overflow with hope by the power of the Holy Spirit. (Romans 15:13)

> We know and rely on the love God has for us. God is love. Whoever lives in love lives in God, and God in them. (1 John 4:16)

> And God is able to bless you abundantly, so that in all things at all times, having all that you need, you will abound in every good work. (2 Corinthians 9:8)

> The creation waits in eager expectation for the children of God to be revealed. For the creation was subjected to frustration, not by its own choice, but by the will of the one who subjected it, in hope that the creation itself will be liberated from its bondage to decay and brought into the freedom and glory of the children of God. (Romans 8:19–21)

Discussion:

Answer the questions to which you relate, being true to your experience. Participation is always voluntary.

1. Have you ever experienced a time when seeing and feeling the wonder, power, and/or beauty of nature overwhelmed or comforted you? Share your experience.
2. In general, how have the ups and downs of life affected you?
3. Can you share a time when going through something difficult helped you grow as a person?
4. Do you believe there is a creator with a plan for humankind, who is active in our lives?
5. What might stop *you* from receiving the love of God and/or the love of the people closest to you?

CHAPTER 3

True Love

The twinkle of the stars, the sparkle of the light upon the water,
the elusive colors of the rainbow—
Reflected light.
We are the light of the world, the warmth of our God.

God is love. —1 John 4:16

I found love with a freckle-faced boy with a shy, yet mischievous smile. We met on the east coast, running into each other far more often than seemed likely. It was a reluctant relationship at first. I longed for connection, having left home at seventeen and wading through some dark waves as I transitioned to adult life. Stephen was one of seven children growing up in the seventies, with dreams of life on a commune, though he was a Catholic boy at heart. Over time, we discovered that we both loved the same music, hiking for hidden waterfalls, and the night life of our small city. We appreciated each other's achievements and found we had similar values and goals. The west coast drew us, and within a few months of each other, we landed in Northern California. On weekends we would drive over the mountains, exploring charming coastal towns—Santa Cruz, Monterey, and Carmel.

That day, I remember, I was wearing a light pink floral sundress. The late afternoon sun was low on the horizon, and we stopped at a mountainside vista. The sunset over the coast was spectacular from above. He looked at me and asked, or rather he stated, "I want to marry you," as though it was a decision he had put a lot of thought into. With all my heart, I wanted to marry him too. It was a commitment you could rest in, and I felt safe.

We married in New England on an autumn day, gathered around the big maple tree where I had played as a child. Color-filled branches were our canopy, and chrysanthemums lined the altar. We declared our love and danced to acoustic guitars, surrounded by family and friends. Soon we were back on the west coast, making a life together. We had children and a home of our own, where we could see the rolling hills. We made plans for the future. Life was good.

Everyone hopes for true love, a love that makes us feel secure and valued. We long for a love we can depend on, shared dreams, and adventure. Stephen and I had a blessed start and the respect we had for each other gave us a strong foundation. Nevertheless, married life takes adjustment, give and take, and learning how to value each other and each other's needs. Navigating life together, growing as a family, is inevitably a time of personal growth as well. We learn the most about ourselves in the midst of our relationships. The first years of married life are especially suited to building character, as well as our bonds. Our concepts of love are put to the test and grow.

For many the fairy-tale idea of happily-ever-after, in this present fallen world, brings disappointment. Relationships inevitably come with conflicts. People are flawed in their attitudes, their thinking, and their histories—bringing it all into the present with a skewed point of view. Loving someone, day by day, is always harder than we think. Having our character stretched is not comfortable. Whether within our marriages, or our relationships with family, friends, and neighbors, to love and accept love can be a challenge. Soon enough we realize that loving someone is not as easy as we thought.

We may *want* to love well, but it's not like we can just snap our fingers or will ourselves to love from the heart. Including the needs of others in our own agendas can be a burden. Sharing each other's dreams means making choices that are different from those we would make alone. With love there is also the possibility of loss. It is a risk as well as a calling. The disappointments of life and relationships hit us hard. Pain and hurt rule us. Misunderstandings and emotions can spiral out of control. Sometimes we even surprise *ourselves* with the intensity of our reactions. Our responses may seem justified in our own eyes, but nothing good comes from them. We learn from experience that love is not easy. Often relationships do not weather the storms to grow stronger.

We are all looking for love we can trust. The truth is, true love is a constant we all have. True love starts with God's love for us and grows in our realization of that great love. Authentic love comes from the very source of true love—our one true God. God loves us like crazy, flaws and all! The love of God for the men and women he created is so great, so deep, *so* beyond our comprehension—but let's try. Think back to a moment in life when you felt deep love for someone—perhaps your wedding day or gazing at an infant child. Or perhaps you can remember a time when you felt loved through and through. Even if you have never felt an overwhelming love, imagine love that deep, and then know it is but a shadow of the amazing love God has for *you*! There is nothing we need to do to be loved by God, and nothing that we *can* do, that anyone can do, will separate us from his love.

> I am convinced that neither death nor life, neither angels nor demons, neither the present nor the future, nor any powers, neither height nor depth, nor anything else in all creation, will be able to separate us from the love of God that is in Christ Jesus our Lord. (Romans 8:38–39)

Take a moment to let this great truth sink in—God loves you! The source of true love is God himself, and he longs to pour out his love into your life and then *through* your life. Your relationship with him is voluntary, or it could not be love, but whatever your response to God's love, his love remains true.

God loves us. This is a constant that cannot be overstated. Whether you believe that or not, whether you trust that is true, can affect your response. God is not above asking for our love. Listen to Jesus's words.

> One of them, an expert in the law, tested him with this question: "Teacher, which is the greatest commandment in the law?" (Matthew 22:35–36)

(It is not Jesus bringing up the law here, but someone who thinks they do a good job keeping it. Jesus's response gets to the heart of the matter.)

> Jesus replied: "'Love the Lord your God with all your heart and with all your soul and with all your mind.' This is the first and greatest commandment." (Matthew 22:37–38)

The creator of heaven and earth asks us to love him! The word for love here is the Greek word *agapao*—the commitment of devotion that is directed by the will but rightfully could be commanded as a duty. Because of who God is—the creator, all-powerful, and the very definition of love— rightfully we should respond in duty with our love in return, and yet he asks us to love him with our heart by choice. The One with the overriding power of the universe allows himself to be vulnerable! He gives us life here on earth as a gift and also the choice to love him as our creator and Father. Can we love God with all our heart, soul, and mind if we never seek to know him? He wants us to learn about true love through his love. He wants us to know him.

> Love is patient, love is kind. It does not envy, it does not boast, it is not proud. It does not dishonor others, it is not self-seeking, it is not easily angered, it keeps no record of wrongs. Love does not delight in evil, but rejoices with the truth. It always protects, always trusts, always hopes, always perseveres. Love never fails. (1 Corinthians 13:4–8)

Wow, this is a description of God's love! It would be wonderful to be loved like this—and we *are* by our creator God. If our marriages reflected this definition of love, we would all live happily-ever-after. I do not measure up to that kind of love! Even when we set our minds to love, often our hearts do not follow. The truth is that God cannot use us to show his love without residing with us, and he cannot reside with us without something being done about our selfish and self-reliant nature. He knows our insecure nature, how we put up walls, how we often hide from him and each other, so he pursues us with passion.

God so loved the world that he gave his one and only Son, that whoever believes in him shall not perish but have eternal life. For God did not send his Son into the world to condemn the world, but to save the world through him. (John 3:16–17)

This is passionate love—God, revealed in the Son, living and dying as man for the purpose of pursuing us! God prepares a loving home for us (John 14:2) and saves us from the sin, lies, and death that can lure us away. *God* was willing to be vulnerable to the attitudes and actions of man for our sake. He was willing to suffer the consequences for the sin of man and the effects of free will. Jesus, our all-powerful creator (John 1:1–4, 9–10), was willing to leave the perfection of heaven so that we could become part of his family. The living God of the universe can now be *with us, personally,* to comfort and empower us with his love. He knows the heartache of this world firsthand. No matter what our past is, he has made it safe to come and receive his amazing, forgiving love. To know the joy of this kind of love is satisfying. Jesus's love has wonderful, eternal returns: "Love never fails" (1 Corinthians 13:8).

God's love never fails, but our love surely does. Let's learn more about how God defines love.

Jesus tells us the most important thing we can do is to love God with all our heart, soul, and mind (Matthew 22:36–38) and continues on:

And the second is like it: "Love your neighbor as yourself." All the Law and the Prophets hang on these two commandments. (Matthew 22:39–40)

Every law and instruction given through God's prophets are summed up here—"Love your neighbor as yourself." Jesus says the first command, about loving God with our complete being, is like the second (also see 1 John 4:20). Bottom line: we demonstrate we love God by loving others. Everything God requires is rooted in love. That's God's heart! "The only thing that counts is faith expressing itself through love" (Galatians 5:6).

The Bible makes it clear that we can be gifted and accomplished, that we can demonstrate faith and sacrifice, but if love is not our guiding motivation, then nothing we do will be of lasting value (1 Corinthians 13:1–3).

There is more to learn about God's love.

These next two truths we really need help with. But don't get discouraged.

To make love possible in our world of free will, forgiveness is essential. God requires that we forgive just as he does, though he knows that is not easy for us. Peter's question is more generous than ours:

> "Lord, how many times shall I forgive my brother or sister who sins against me? Up to seven times?"
>
> Jesus answered, "Not seven times, but seventy-seven times." (Matthew 18:21–22)

The Parable of the Unmerciful Servant, Matthew 18:21–35, echoes Jesus's teaching in the Lord's Prayer. If we are unwilling to forgive others from our heart, forgiveness from God is hampered, and our relationship with him is affected (Matthew 6:12, 14–15). God has complete confidence that his love will enable us to forgive others, if we are willing to accept it. Even our prayers are affected if we harbor unforgiveness in our hearts (Mark 11:25). God forgave and will forgive us so much; he asks us to reflect his character by doing the same.

Forgiveness in our relationships can start even before the offender is sorry and the relationship is restored. We free ourselves by having the humility to forgive within our hearts and love others just the way they are. Full restoration and healing in relationships come with the offender's humility. When those who have done harm (many times both parties play a role) are truly sorry, ask forgiveness, and move forward with loving action, then trust is reestablished. When we mess up, we can talk to God about it, listen to his still voice, and admit our mistakes. Accepting the gift of his forgiveness helps us take the necessary steps forward. The grace and love we show toward others, within healthy boundaries, can help bring them to regret harmful attitudes and actions and seek God's help. Receiving God's forgiveness and grace empowers change.

As God empowers us to forgive, there emerges something otherwise impossible—peace. Peace with God, with ourselves, with our family and friends, and even more.

"You have heard that it was said, 'Love your neighbor and hate your enemy.' But I tell you, love your enemies and pray for those who persecute you, that you may be children of your Father in heaven. He causes his sun to rise on the evil and the good, and sends rain on the righteous and the unrighteous. If you love those who love you, what reward will you get? … And if you greet only your own people, what are you doing more than others?" (Matthew 5:43–47)

I've always believed God will bless those who do good (Hebrews 6:10), but he also sends blessings to those who don't. The verse above tells us God gives blessings to both the loving and unloving, but his amazing family rewards are for those who learn to love like him. Could he want to use *us* to bless someone who has wronged us? Does he want us to love them? Clearly the answer is *yes*! That is hard—hard for us to get our heads around. It is hard to accept within our hearts. If we could love our enemies, valuing their needs as much as we do our own, it would break down misconceptions and give peace a chance. But that is really hard. The whole of the Old Testament shows that we could not become people of righteousness, which means people of love, on our own, no matter how we tried. God knows that in our own strength we will fail to meet his standard of love. That is why he came to earth. Jesus came in order for us to have the help we need to act in true love—a sacrificial love. He came to save the world!

When the kindness and love of God our Savior appeared, he saved us, not because of righteous things we had done, but because of his mercy. He saved us through the washing of rebirth and renewal by the Holy Spirit, whom he poured out on us generously through Jesus Christ our Savior, so that, having been justified by his grace, we might become heirs having the hope of eternal life. This is a trustworthy saying. And I want you to stress these things, so that those who have trusted in God may be careful to devote themselves to doing what is good.

These things are excellent and profitable for *everyone*.
(Titus 3:4–8, italics added)

As we learn about what God's idea of true love is, we start to realize just how far short we fall. Yet God loves us unconditionally. He will stand with us in our struggle. Are you mindful of any area or relationships that could be improved or healed? Don't be afraid to ask God for his help. I believe that learning to love is the purpose of our life journey.

The love of God for the men, women, and children of this world is beyond our comprehension. God is the source of true love. He wants to give us the help we need to live well, and he paid a high price to make that possible. Fame or fortune will not last, but God's love is eternal.

Once I had a house in the California foothills and a young family just learning to love. We could not see what the future held. I did not know the width and depth of true love. Those first years of marriage had taught me lessons in love, but I had much more to learn. There is a bountiful plan, far beyond what we understand. God's plan of love stretches throughout eternity and weaves together humanity. He is present in life's joys and life's hardships. Life is an invitation to the journey of learning to love. It is not a journey we can take alone.

We know and rely on the love God has for us. God is love. Whoever lives in love, lives in God, and God in them. This is how love is made complete among us so that we will have confidence on the day of judgment: In this world we are like Jesus. There is no fear in love. (1 John 4:16–18)

See what great love the Father has lavished on us, that we should be called children of God! And that is what we are! The reason the world does not know us is that it did not know him. (1 John 3:1)

The fruit of the Spirit is love, joy, peace, forbearance, kindness, goodness, faithfulness, gentleness and self-control. Against such things there is no law. (Galatians 5:22–23)

Let no debt remain outstanding, except the continuing debt to love one another, for whoever loves others has fulfilled the law. The commandments, "You shall not commit adultery," "You shall not murder," "You shall not steal," "You shall not covet," and whatever other command there may be, are summed up in this one command: "Love your neighbor as yourself." Love does no harm to a neighbor. Therefore love is the fulfillment of the law. (Romans 13:8–10)

Discussion:

1. Have you ever experienced a time when you felt God's love or presence?
2. Do you find it challenging to consider the needs of others equally as important as your own?
3. In learning about God's definition of love, what made an impression on you?
4. Did you ever have an unrealistic view about love that led to disappointment?
5. Read 1 John 4:7–21 together. What stands out to you in this passage?
   a. Where does love come from?
   b. What is the evidence of our relationship with God?
   c. How is God's love made complete in us?
   d. Why does perfect love drive out fear?

CHAPTER 4

Our Plans

Plans we make,
But we cannot see.
On the road ahead,
What our role will be.

We are God's masterpiece. He has created us anew in
Christ Jesus, so we can do the good things he planned
for us long ago.

—Ephesians 2:10 NLT

"I'm planning to take the kids to the zoo today." I said, reaching for little
Jeff, as he clung to Stephen.

"Daddy …" Jeff pleaded. He did not want him to leave!

Stephen had been finishing a big project at work and had put in some
long hours that week. He hated to leave little Jeff. He genuinely loved
playing with his babies and planning special outings. As a matter of fact,
we were are all going to Lake Tahoe that weekend. He gave his little two-
year-old a big hug, assuring him he would be home that evening and have
lots of time to play—that we had lots of fun ahead of us. I held on to Jeff
so Stephen could get out the door.

I sat on the back-porch steps later that afternoon, looking out over
his garden, hoping he would come. A voice on the phone had told me to
come to the hospital. I had heard the officer tell me someone had died, as
I sat stopped in a line of traffic at the tragic intersection. I had waited for

what seemed like ages for someone to come and talk with me. I'd insisted on seeing him, on holding his bloodstained body one last time. But still, I could not believe he was gone. That afternoon I waited for him in his garden, but he never came. I looked for him, but he was not there. In an instant our whole world changed.

Stephen died suddenly at twenty-nine. All of our life plans were falling away, like the leaves on a windy autumn day, though it was still spring. I held on to the hope that I would see him again … at some elusive time, a lifespan away. My life had shattered, yet I had to get up. I needed to care for our babies. No longer would I see the joyful smiles that their precious lives brought him.

I believed God loved us, but yet our world was filled with sorrow. My children needed their father! I longed for my best friend and wanted to be held. As the first year passed, my little boy was sad, worried that he was forgetting his dad, so like the scene in *Sleepless in Seattle*. Baby Hannah had been only ten months old and would never know him. Their loss broke my heart—a heart that was already crushed because he was gone. As time passed the children wished for a father and suggested we could buy one at the store. There must be a way to ease the longing.

I married again, two years later. Michael was an attractive young man, an engineer, who had an element of mystery about him. Most pleasing was that he loved my little ones and that they loved him. He enjoyed hearing their laughter, as he tickled them or tossed them in the air. They could not get enough of having a playful male personality come by from time to time. We planned a trip to Minnesota to meet his family. While there, we were wed at his family home. His uncle was the pastor who married us.

God had answered my prayer. But not as I had expected.

The children and I had moved across country, back to New England, to have the support of family. Now we were moving again, to Florida, because my new husband had taken a new job. I wanted him to find a job he liked, but not so far away. Everything was happening so fast! We were not communicating, and he seemed distant. This was not what I had hoped for.

Once we were in Florida, my grief surfaced, coming like a wave, no longer able to be contained. I had been trying to hide it, but decided

I needed to confide in Michael. His response was what I feared: "It's been over two years. By now you should be over it." *I wish I could be!* I reasoned; it would be hard to marry a widow, so I decided to do my best not to speak of Stephen. Instead of finding the healing I was looking for, my pain increased.

Our relationship was in retreat. I realized my new husband, by personality, was a loner. My heart ached, to the point of being physically painful. I sank to the cold floor and cried out to God in my pain. Why did I marry again, only to feel more alone than ever? God's comfort washed over me. His love held me. A ray of light streamed from the window.

God assured me and whispered, "Love him."

But how! How could I love a man who seemed to reject me at every turn? *But, but I need to be loved!*

"I love you," God whispered.

I felt it. He helped me get up and wipe away my tears. The school bus was coming soon. I began to breathe, gathered little Hannah, and soon was outside, smiling as my little boy climbed down the big steps. We were both coming home to love. I desperately hung on to my hope: *God has a plan for good.*

Our plans don't go as we imagine. Shaken or frustrated, we face emerging realities. Our world of wonder is also full of hardship. Along with the good, no one escapes the effects of evil. We face hard and frustrating work in life (Genesis 3:17–19). There is frustration in our relationships. With mankind's free choice also came sin. Death was allowed, so we would not live endlessly in a world of pain and disappointment (Genesis 3:22–24). And with death comes sorrow. Yet, even within these difficult and uncertain dynamics, nothing is a surprise to God. Though God is never the cause of evil in our lives, he may not intervene. He allows it. Nevertheless, God has promised that he will not abandon us, but wants to help us through.

No matter what our problems or pain, God longs to meet our deepest needs. God knows when and where we have been hurt and he longs to heal us. This world of free will is full of loss and disappointment; God knows and he is there for us. We're busy with this and with that, so he patiently waits for us. Often it is in times of trial and conflict—when we are at the end of our control—that we experience the reality of our invisible God. In moments of brokenness, God meets us. He has an all-encompassing plan to rescue and heal us from sin and pain—a plan that weaves our lives together. No matter what life or evil sends our way, God promises that if we look to him, he will work things out for good (Romans 8:28). Not just good for others, but good for us.

Initially it is hard to trust God, as we mourn over disappointments, lost dreams, or the people we love. But then, as we turn to him, we experience the unexpected. He provides our needs and gives us flashes of hope. Resting in the love we receive from God, we find comfort and purpose; we change and grow. God's love begins to heal us at the center of our being, so we can venture out to focus on others.

With hardship, we look for purpose through a new lens. Our struggle brings awareness. Often, we develop empathy, becoming more sensitive to the plight of others. Steps of love guard our heart against bitterness. Our capacity to love grows, and our plans change. God's love flows through us. This kind of love takes people by surprise. *How refreshing that someone is taking a genuine interest in me. How unexpected that someone shows love to me, when I have hurt them. How steadfast to serve in the midst of such difficulty and danger.* The lens of true love places great value on others. It is patient and kind, never prideful, always protects, and seeks the truth. God's plan has a meaningful role for those who see more clearly.

We all have plans for the future and hopes we dream to fulfill. Nevertheless, I have realized there is a bigger plan, one that takes into account the tragedies and the pain; a plan that weaves our lives together, as if time did not exist; a plan that considers both good and evil, in our world of free will. In the realities of our world, there are times when it's hard to go on. But then, as we turn to God, revealing our inner hearts to him, there is comfort and light, a glimmer of hope. God has a plan for us. It's a new plan, with enlightened dreams. It may not be easy, but it's absolutely good!

> Many are the plans in a person's heart,
>   but it is the LORD's purpose that prevails.
> (Proverbs 19:21)

"I know the plans I have for you," says the Lord. "They are plans for good and not for disaster, to give you a future and a hope. In those days when you pray, I will listen. If you look for me wholeheartedly, you will find me. (Jeremiah 29:13 NLT)

But do not forget this one thing, dear friends: With the Lord a day is like a thousand years and a thousand years are like a day. (2 Peter 3:8)

But the plans of the LORD stand firm forever,
    the purposes of his heart through all generations.
(Psalms 33:11)

Discussion:

1. Have you had plans for your life that were changed by fate?
2. Read the Parable of the Good Samaritan in Luke 10:25–37.
    a. What law, did Jesus say, must be kept to receive eternal life?
    a. The story is told to answer what question?
    a. Which two people in the parable had their plans changed?
    a. Was the change in plans by choice or by fate?
    a. Who in the story was unwilling to change their plans?
3. Has there ever been a time in your life when unexpected circumstances helped you grow?
4. Have your hopes and dreams changed over time? How?

CHAPTER 5

We Can Do It

I tried and tried to climb that wall,
To pick you up, when you had a fall.
But it seemed, I never reached the goal,
I am not enough to make us whole.

I don't really understand myself, for I want to
do what is right, but I don't do it.
—Romans 7:15 NLT

There is a long list that I believed I could accomplish—for starters, be a talented architect, an amazing parent and run a successful business. (You can see that I have a healthy dose of ego, along with my insecurities.) I believed that if I was a good wife, then our family would be happy. God wanted me to love my new husband and I set my mind to do it, believing I could love well and save the relationship. I set out to do my part to save our world as well. There was confidence in my head, but I lost it in my heart. As the reality of life set in, so did disappointment. I spent my life striving, never quite reaching my goals.

I can hear the little mice singing in the Disney animated classic *Cinderella*, "We can do it, we can do it …" as they go about sewing a dress for sweet Cinderella. They use cast-off scraps and beads so Cinderella would have something to wear; they hoped she could go to the ball. Cinderella's mother and father had died and the people she lived with did not love her and treated her unkindly. Yet, she has been a faithful and loving sister—obeying and serving through all kinds of injustice. The mice create a lovely dress for Cinderella, only to have the evil stepsisters tear it to shreds as soon as they see it.

Life is hard! Life is unfair! Even if we set out to be good people, most of us don't react well to injustice. You can hear children in every household cry out, "That's not fair!" Will we love our enemies? Can we fight for justice without succumbing to violence? Will we keep believing and persevere? Cinderella's song is from the heart: "When your heart is grieving, if you just keep believing." Our faithful reaction is key, as the universal story teaches. Then, something wonderful happens for Cinderella; something she could not do on her own. The fairy godmother steps in, providing a beautiful, enchanting gown, dressing her like the daughter of a king, a daughter of God.

> I delight greatly in the LORD;
>   my soul rejoices in my God.
> For he has clothed me with garments of salvation
>   and arrayed me in a robe of his righteousness,...
> (Isaiah 61:10)

Being made ready for a world beyond is possible for us too. Belief that God is faithful and good, even when our hearts are grieving, is proven true throughout our life experience. As we overcome trials, we learn we can trust God and begin to recognize that our journey has purpose. We become transformed into people who reflect God's image.

There is a truth God teaches us that is a long, hard lesson. It is a truth illustrated through all the years of the Old Testament, though God planned for the solution right from the beginning. It is a truth that every major religion comes up against. As hard as we try to follow God's rules for success, we mess up. We always fall short. We try to have loving relationships, yet many relationships fall apart. We plan and work to reach our dreams and be successful, yet ultimately, we can't even take our next breath without God's help. He is the sustainer of life and the source of purpose. We can work hard, but without God's protection and blessings, everything can just as easily be torn apart. And God allows it! He allows the battle, the struggle, to help us. He allows hardship and failure, for without them we cannot mature. Our will alone is not enough to meet our dreams for true love and success. We need God's involvement in every aspect of our lives, but often don't acknowledge it. We need God's provision—food, clothing, a job, etc. We need God's help to do the right thing in our actions and relationships. We need God's truth to open our eyes and move us forward. We need his help to forgive and receive forgiveness. We need God's direction and involvement to make a lasting impact with our lives. God is the source of love that's from the heart.

In the Old Testament God made a series of promises that were conditional. God promised his people blessings for their obedience. They were to love God and each other and follow the rules he had set in place for their protection and good. Over and over the people said, "We can do it!" (Exodus 24:3, 7 and Joshua 24:16, 21, 24). In Exodus 24:3 they say, "Everything the Lord has said, we will do," but they never could. They tried, but before long they always went astray.

This was no surprise to God. At the same time that he gave the rules to follow, he also gave instructions for what to do when the rules were broken. Once a year, they had a Day of Atonement. This was a day of mercy for all the disobedience of God's people; it was a day to be reconciled to God. On this day two goats were brought to Aaron, the priest. One goat was sacrificed for the sin of the nation. "But the goat chosen by lot as the scapegoat shall be presented alive before the Lord to be used for making atonement by sending it into the desert as the scapegoat" (Leviticus 16:10). The priest placed his two hands on the head of the second goat and pronounced each and every sin of the entire nation upon him. A trustworthy man took the goat far into the wilderness, so it could never return to camp. If only we could send away all the bad stuff, every mistake we have ever made.

Good news: The scapegoat is a picture of God's plan.

> The Lord is merciful and loving,
>> slow to become angry and full of constant love.
> He does not keep on rebuking;
>> he is not angry forever.
> He does not punish us as we deserve
>> or repay us according to our sins and wrongs.

As high as the sky is above the earth,
    so great is his love for those who honor him.
As far as the east is from the west,
    so far does he remove our sins from us.
As a father is kind to his children,
    so the LORD is kind to those who honor him.
(Psalm 103:8-13 GNB)

We know that in all things God works for the good of those who love him, who have been called according to his purpose. (Romans 8:28)

Be joyful in hope, patient in affliction, faithful in prayer. (Romans 12:12)

Discussion:

1. Have you had dreams that were not obtained or goals you did not reach?
2. Were you able to move forward from disappointment? How?
3. State one of the overall principles illustrated throughout the Old Testament.
4. Identify a situation in your life in which you need to depend on God.
5. Are there any areas in which you continually struggle?
6. Are there situations or relationships in your life in which you wish you had a second chance?
7. What do you think the Day of Atonement symbolizes?

CHAPTER 6

Spirit of Truth

It seems truth plays hide-and-seek with me.
Yet the One who made me, knows me,
And sees all sides—true reality.
He knows the truth, do I?
He loves, can I?

Then you will know the truth, and the truth will set you
free.

—John 8:32

Truth is the lens of enlightenment. Truth is more valuable than we realize
and harder to know than we recognize. We are not very good at seeing,
hearing, or acting upon the truth. It's easy to lie to ourselves, and to
be misled—teenagers who think they can handle a sketchy situation,
overloaded adults who tell themselves everything is fine, financially
struggling people who buy what they don't need on easy credit. Life is
a maze of subtle lies that play with our minds and lead us to dead-end
places. We easily stray from the path of reality—the path that will lead us
to a free and joyful life.

By nature, I am optimistic. I have always thought of positive thinking
as a strength, but I've learned it can also be a weakness. At times my rose-
colored outlook, allows me to hide from the truth. It's so much easier to
gloss over problems than to deal with them head on. Sometimes, it's good

to smooth things over, let things go, or believe everything will be all right, but at other times it's unhealthy and even irresponsible.

Relationships need truth.

Michael and I had become like two ships passing in the night. He lived in his world, and I lived in mine. Our unwillingness to face the problems in our marriage, had a negative impact on the entire family. I pushed down my true feelings, for the sake of "peace," but was I at peace? The lies in our lives come in many ways, often not straightforward. Whether we see things with a positive or negative view, rarely do we perceive the total reality of a situation. Intentional or unintentional, subtle lies affect the quality of our lives.

The lack of truth is where everything falls apart. Healthy lives and relationships need truth like a garden needs water, but there is a big problem—we are not very good at truth! To see and hear reality, to know the truth, is challenging. We often make bad decisions, based on our distorted view, not able to see the big picture or even tomorrow. Our perceived reality is rarely true reality. We see other people with a distorted view, often not recognizing their value. We don't even see ourselves clearly—too hard on ourselves in one area and too easy in another. Even with a high regard for truth, we often don't know the truth or tell the whole truth. Then there are all the people who have little regard for the truth, who lie to avoid consequences, to manipulate, or to profit. We start to get a glimpse of how deceptive our world is. We may fight for justice, but we make mistakes, and so people are in prison who did not commit the crime, and the guilty may still walk free. We think we solve a problem, such as getting from here to there in fossil-fueled cars, only later to discover we created a bigger problem. We must admit, it is a challenge, perhaps impossible, for us to see the big picture. Only God himself knows the whole truth. Of course, that shouldn't stop us from doing our best to tell the truth and seek it. Facts matter. We need to look for truth, that's for sure!

The truth will ultimately set us free (John 8:32), if we are willing to find it and face it, but that's not easy. Few of us really believe that the truth *will* set us free. People can lie more easily than they think. Curiosity. discovery.com reports on the question: *How often does the average person lie?*

Some people lie all the time—for compulsive liars, telling a falsehood is a default action. But for a stab at a more reasonable number, we can look at a study conducted by University of Massachusetts researcher Robert Feldman, which demonstrates how reflexive the act of lying is for many people. In the study, which was published in the Journal of Basic and Applied Psychology, Feldman and his team of researchers asked two strangers to talk for 10 minutes. The conversations were recorded, and then each subject was asked to review the tape. Before looking at the footage, the subjects told researchers that they had been completely honest and accurate in their statements, but once the tape rolled, the subjects were amazed to discover all the little lies that came out in just 10 minutes. According to Feldman, 60 percent of the subjects lied at least once during the short conversation, and in that span of time, subjects told an average of 2.92 false things ....
In studies in which children have been observed in social interactions, 4-year-olds fibbed at least once every two hours, while six-year-olds could only make it 90 minutes before spinning a falsehood.

Pairs of strangers who engaged in conversation were amazed at how many times they were not accurate in their statements. "Most people lie in everyday conversation when they are trying to appear likable or competent," according to Feldman's study. It is more difficult than we admit, even to ourselves, to tell the truth, yet our truthful and encouraging words are just what our world needs. It is natural for us to focus on ourselves and therefore try to build ourselves up in the eyes of others, yet God wants us to be humble and focus on the interests of others (Philippians 2:3–8). We can see from this report that being completely truthful does not come naturally.

With truth comes freedom. Yet, there is a world of lies seducing us from the truth, and lies never lead us to what we are longing for. We are more vulnerable to the deception in this world than we realize. In contrast, God knows the truth (1 Samuel 2:3), he tells the truth (Titus 1:2), and he is active in revealing truth (John 16:13). God is just (Romans 3:5–6) and faithful to keep his promises in the light of eternity (Hebrews 10:23). God is truthful!

Many believe our internal conscience is one proof of God. How can we understand the concept of yes and no, right and wrong, or truth and lies? When we tell a child no, they soon realize they need to be tricky in order to get their way. They have a look of guilt on their face when they are caught. Our moral compass is not trustworthy; it's broken, skewed toward ourselves, but it is still there. Our intellectual design enables us to understand right from wrong and have the ability to seek truth.

Truth helps us make good decisions. God is a good decision maker, because he knows the full truth and always acts in love. Sometimes we question that, because we are incapable of seeing the full scope of history and future eternity. There are happenings beyond our field of vision. God understands people's limits and doubts, yet calls us to trust him. Our experiences teach us that our trust is sound. His decisions are always based on justice and love (2 Thessalonians 1:6; 1 John 4:8). That's how he asks us to make our decisions in this world—with truth and with love.

In opposition, bad, deceiving influences are also vying to impact the decisions that affect what we say and do. In the battle between good and evil, attacking truth is the first line of offence. It started with Adam and Eve when the serpent asked, *"Did God really say,* 'You must not eat from any tree in the garden'?" First, he twisted the truth, as it was just one tree they were told not to eat from, and then he lied about God's intent. The evil serpent charged, *God doesn't want you to know everything as he does.* God wanted to protect, but the serpent claimed *he is keeping wisdom from them* (see Genesis 3:1–7). Evil starts with a twisting of truth and then comes in for the kill with outright lies. Evil aims for us to doubt God's love and doubt his word, ultimately breaking our trust in God. The same is true today.

To see and act on truth, we need God's help. He promises to guide us when we turn to him. He desires to reveal truth. God wants us to know how much we are loved and that we can fully trust him. This truth is the cornerstone for loving relationships. Evil aims to prevent that trust, but God intervenes.

Jesus said, "If you love me, keep my commands. *And* I will ask the

Father, and he will give you another advocate to help you and be with you forever—the Spirit of truth" (John 14:15–17, italics added). We show God we love him by keeping his commands, but we know humans are historically not good at loving others as much as themselves. *"And"*—to enable this, Jesus has asked the Father, on our behalf, for a helper, our advocate, to be with us. He was willing to cover humanity's sin, at a great cost, in order to give us the help we need to combat the lies that surround us.

One of the ways God communicates to us is through our conscience. He reveals truth—positive truths of encouragement and also where we have gone wrong or have a bad attitude. Often, we are unwilling to acknowledge it. We do not except his love. We don't want to hear where we have gone wrong. Yet this is the first step in getting the help we need. God never falsely accuses as evil does (Revelation 12:9–10). God never convicts us of guilt to keep us feeling guilty (that is never God) but rather so that we may receive his forgiveness and move forward in his love. God shows us who we really are, hoping we are humble enough to acknowledge the areas we need help with. He loves us and wants our best, and so he helps us see the truth about ourselves. When we choose to do wrong or act unlovingly, he makes us aware through our thoughts. How we respond affects how well we hear God next time. If we harden our hearts, it affects our conscience.

The first step in asking for help is to know that we need it. Many people try to do the right thing (though still sometimes fail). Others don't really care. Some people fool themselves, convincing themselves the wrong they are doing is right. Others seek to deceive and destroy. No matter which categories we fall into, we are all separated from God because of our nature, prone to sin (Isaiah 59:2; Romans 3:23). He is the very source of good and truth, and though he draws us, we shrink back and disengage because of our guilt and a false sense of self-protection. This separation even leads many to believe there is no God. God gave us this world to take care of, but we have made a mess of it, just as we often make a mess of our relationships with our family, friends, and neighbors. Ultimately, we hurt ourselves, as well as those around us. The longer we fight the truth, the harder we become. Deceptive thoughts from within, and the lies of the world, keep us lost and alone, feeding the chaos of our lives. We need a trusting relationship with the God who created us, yet we are separated from him. Do you feel it?

Our separation from God is a big problem, and Jesus came to solve it! He came in a most unexpected way—as a baby: his human mother a young virgin girl named Mary, and his Father the Spirit of God (Luke 1:26–38). He is both the Son of God and the Son of Man, which he often called himself. Jesus, who always was, came from heaven to earth to give us the help we so desperately needed. Please understand, sin causes the death of everything—relationships, our hopes and dreams, and the physical death of our aging bodies. God cannot allow sin to continue forever. He is both just to punish sin and incredibly compassionate—and so Jesus came.

As God, Jesus's perfection enabled him to live as a man without ever doing wrong. Therefore, as man, he could pay for humanity's sin as a perfect Messiah (Savior), something we could never do for ourselves. No matter where you are from or what your religion, Jesus came to provide peace with God for you. Jesus willingly suffered and died on a cross to take the punishment for the whole world's sin! God himself broke the ultimate power of sin and death in our lives and rose again to life after three days. Jesus upheld justice by paying sin's ultimate cost to set us free! He endured it all for the *joy* (Hebrews 12:2) of seeing us reconciled to Father God and the *joy* of seeing his children reach out to one another in truth and love— the joy of providing us a way home. God's compassionate promise of hope was put into action.

If we acknowledge his great gift, and accept it for ourselves, we can be saved from our sin and receive eternal life. It is then that God credits us with what we will be in eternity—pure and sinless men and women. Therefore, God himself can reside within us, ending our separation! The Spirit of truth (Spirit of God) can now personally guide us and help us to find truth. He is our eternal advocate—the one Jesus promised. When we acknowledge and yield to the Spirit of truth, he can empower us to truly love others. "The fruit of the Spirit is love, joy, peace, forbearance, kindness, goodness, faithfulness, gentleness and self-control" (Galatians 5:22–23). God longs to have a relationship with us, as a wise and caring Father and give us an advocate to help us. God offers to be our companion, friend, and teacher through Jesus and the Spirit of truth.

Some readers may find it confusing when we talk about the Father

God, Jesus (Son of God, Son of Man), and the Holy Spirit of truth, so let's take a moment to clarify. There is **one** (Deuteronomy 6:4; Mark 12:29; Galatians 3:20) holy, perfect, good, all-knowing, powerful, and loving God. To accomplish his purposes, God reveals himself as three persons (Matthew 28:19; 1 Peter 1:2; John 10:30), and God can do this all at the same time. The roles of our triune God cannot be entirely separated, but to help us grasp the concept we can make some distinctions. Our Father God is reigning over all the earth with goodness, wisdom, and power (Psalm 8; 147:1–11). Jesus, his only Son, came to earth to teach us, to show us God's character (Mark 10:1; John 10:30), to be our example, and to save us from our sin (John 3:16–17). Jesus came to end our separation from God, and he now intercedes for us (Romans 8:34–39). Jesus will eventually judge us (John 5:22). The Holy Spirit of truth guides us to conviction and truth, providing us comfort and healing as he dwells within us. He directs us daily as we allow him (John 14:16–18; Romans 8:1–28).

In unity, God created the universe and you and me. (Did you know plural pronouns are used for God throughout the creation account, found in the book of Genesis?) God the Father, Jesus, and the Spirit of truth are one, entirely, as 1x1x1=1. Perfect unity in character and mission may help to explain part of the complexity of *one God* revealed in three persons. It may be hard for us to absorb, but don't let that get in the way of your belief. Consider all the mysteries of nature and our advanced technological world that we find difficult to understand. God's thoughts, intellect, and plans are infinitely beyond ours (Isaiah 55:9)! How then, can mere mortals understand the whole of our majestic God? Yet through God's word, and also our experience, he teaches us that he is the Father, Son, and Holy Spirit (the Trinity), the *one true God*.

Faith in Jesus, reconciling us to Father God, is available to everyone (John 14:6; 2 Peter 3:9). Becoming his follower, is a decision that should not be taken lightly. It is acknowledging we cannot pay for our own sin, apart from Jesus's perfect sacrifice. He was our scapegoat, carrying our sin upon himself. Doing good cannot cover our personal sin before God (Romans 3:20–26). Only Jesus, takes our sin away (Matthew 26:28; Acts 4:12; Hebrews 10:14–18). As we trust Jesus, our sin is covered by his willing sacrifice, and therefore, the Holy Spirit of truth can reside within us!

(God's Spirit could not and cannot reside with those who are unrepentant or trust themselves to be holy before our holy all-powerful God.)

When we accept Jesus's gift, we become his brothers and sisters (Hebrews 2:11). That comes along with accepting the Father's authority in our lives, just as Jesus does. It is the start of a relationship with our *Abba* father, God. *Abba* is a name that shows his affection for us. He invites us to become his sons and daughters (Romans 8:14–16), trusting him to give us instructions for good, as our loving Father. Choosing to follow Jesus, is accepting God's love *and* his authority, learning to trust that he is always interested in our growth and well-being.

The death and resurrection of Jesus brought about the time in history when God can direct our lives in a very personal way to accomplish his compassionate plan. In Old Testament times (before Jesus came), it was rare to have God's Spirit, the Spirit of truth, with a human. These chosen few were called the anointed or the prophets, because they were led by God, were taught truth, and sometimes knew the future. These truths were revealed to them through God's Spirit or voice. They were God's chosen to lead and speak to his creation.

Now, ever since the arrival of the Spirit of truth to believers (recorded in Acts 2), everyone has the opportunity to be directed by the same Spirit as Moses, Elijah, or David. As with them, we need to cooperate with God, so that he can work with us and through us as we learn to love. When he corrects or directs us, we need to respond in order to keep the relationship growing. Learning to hear God's direction comes with experience, as we are still in a dangerously misleading world. As we respond and mature, with the help of the Spirit of truth, we become able to recognize God's voice.

So how do we receive and cooperate with the Spirit of truth? God knows each of us better than we know ourselves. He wants us to get to know him through a heartfelt loving relationship. He is patient, wanting no one to perish but all to repent and accept his gift of love (2 Peter 3:9). If we turn to God and thankfully accept the gift of what Jesus has done to pay for our sin, we can have the Holy Spirit living with us, giving us comfort, confidence, and determination guided by love. "For the Spirit God gave us does not make us timid, but gives us power, love and self-discipline" (2 Timothy 1:7). We cannot see the Holy Spirit of truth, but we can begin to know him as we trust him day by day. God is active in the situations of our lives, helping us to follow his ways and do his will. In our hearts and minds, he calls us.

We discover what is best for our lives by listening and, most important, by obeying (Matthew 7:7–12). He wants to give us a variety of good gifts, teaching us to love. Jesus was our example; when he walked on this earth, he relied entirely on the Father. When the religious leaders questioned the source of his authority, "Jesus gave them this answer 'Very truly I tell you, the Son can do nothing by himself; he can do only what he sees his Father doing, because whatever the Father does the Son also does'" (John 5:19). The Spirit of truth helps us see what God is doing. He guides us and helps us do his will. It is not a one-time decision to cooperate with the Spirit of truth, but rather it is a lifestyle of commitment that affects decisions we make throughout each day. Will we cooperate with the Spirit of truth or go our own way? Everybody wants their life to make a difference and to be a part of something lasting and good. Jesus said in John 15:5, "Apart from me you can do nothing." Jesus showed us that he relies on his relationship with the Father, and we need to rely on Jesus and the Spirit of truth, who are our connection to the Father as well.

Many people are skeptical for a variety of reasons. Nature calls us to the truth, but evil calls us to doubt. God has told us that not everyone who claims to hear from the Spirit of truth is authentic (2 Peter 2:1). Observe those who mirror God's love (1 John 4). Ask what motivates them to love sacrificially. Evil has influenced many people to believe God does not exist or is untrustworthy, because they have been disillusioned by those who talk of God but don't walk in love. We are all vulnerable to make mistakes (as God's voice is usually not audible), and we are all learning; however, God's followers learn to admit their mistakes and engage to develop a loving heart. They are people who trust Jesus and demonstrate faith, by using their God-given gifts and abilities on behalf of others—to extend his love through their actions, resources, encouragement, and prayers (James 1:19–27; 2:14–25; 4:17; 5:13). It is then that our life stories, and the true stories of God's love throughout history, are received with their rightful credibility.

Talking and listening to God—prayer—is a part of developing our relationship with him as he guides us to know truth. It doesn't need to be out loud, but talk to God. Reveal to God your innermost thoughts and feelings. Express your thankfulness for the beauty that touches you—through nature, acts of love, or blessings large and small. Ask forgiveness when you make mistakes and for help to go forward with love. Prayer plays a role in learning truth—receiving comfort, understanding, and instruction. Ask for wisdom in the situations of life; then listen and watch for God to reveal new insight. Through reading God's word, the tested input of other believers, and providential circumstances, the Spirit of truth communicates and directs us. God's direction is never contrary to the precepts of his word, the Bible—God's word is our foundation.

Prayer invites God to be active in people's lives; it is evidence that we trust and depend on him. Our hopes are realized and power is unleashed for good in this world as we call upon God, making ourselves available and trusting his guidance. He even orchestrates the happenings in our lives to put us in the time and place where he can teach us truth, use us for good, or give us the flashes of hope we need. We learn to respond to his "still small voice" as we sense and confirm his direction in our lives. It is a practical matter, because we don't know the inside story. God helps us see more clearly. We may not recognize a lack of love in our own hearts, but God can gently correct us, and as we become willing to change, he gives us his peace. We cannot fully know the hearts of those around us, their lives, emotions, thoughts, hurts, or motives. We can only observe clues, but God knows fully each individual and what's happening around us, so we can trust him for guidance to take the right actions. Pouring out our heart to God, asking for his guidance and listening, is practical and necessary in order to change within and also to reach out in a way that affects the truth of each situation.

We experience his intervention and direction in tangible ways. He gives us the wisdom and the help we need to act in love. Our faith grows, and so do we, as we respond to God's voice as he "speaks" to us through our conscience, his people, circumstances, and his word. Will we listen and respond? Will we change our attitudes when we feel that gentle correction, or is it going to take something more? Will we desire to be part of his family, enough to give up our control and allow him access to our lives? Will we get involved in the lives of others when he prompts us to or turn the other way?

We can trust God. But by nature we don't, and so we must learn to trust him, day by day, moment by moment. My father found it intimidating to go to church. At times I went my own way, making decisions that did not honor God. Michael is from a family of missionaries and pastors, yet he has found it difficult to depend on God or to hear God's voice. Nevertheless, God did not give up on any of us. Jesus said, "The Son of Man came to seek and to save the lost" (Luke 19:10). We are all lost without God's help, no matter where we come from. He wants to make us aware of the truth and show us the way. God wants to teach us to recognize his voice. No matter what family we are from, we can become part of God's family. If we are willing to accept Jesus's sacrificial gift and give him our lives, God promises to never leave us or forsake us (Deuteronomy 31:8; Matthew 28:20; Hebrews 13:5). Allowing God to change us, to move us, and to help us, as he teaches us to navigate life with patience and love, is evidence that our faith is real. It is evidence that we value truth.

She Listened

Michael's parents retired to a cabin on the birch-lined lakeshores of Minnesota. One morning, as his mom looked out at the lake, she kept having the repeated thought and feeling that her neighbors nearby needed her. They were an elderly couple, the man in his eighties. Cathy picked up the phone and called to discover that he was sobbing. It turned out that his wife, who suffered from kidney failure, was in a hospital in North Dakota, three hours away. Cathy had not known. He longed to be with his wife, but could not drive.

She could help! Cathy told him to pack a bag. She would be there in an hour to take him to the hospital. Joy and relief flooded him as he realized he could be by his sick wife's side. His visit lifted his wife's spirits, and she soon got well enough to come home for a time. Ever since, he calls Cathy his angel. She had listened to God's still voice and had taken action.

Why Didn't I Listen?

I didn't listen, and my heart began to break. Like many teens, I went through an awkward stage—thick glasses, braces, and a funny but mean nickname. When it came to boys, I felt very insecure. In my sophomore year of high school, a junior boy actually asked *me* out! I believed I would follow God's rules when it came to dating. I believed in remaining sexually pure until marriage, but a year passed, and I was put to the test. I began to *think* that if I wanted to keep my boyfriend, I needed to make him happy by having sex. *If I say no, he will be disappointed and upset. I may lose him. He gave me a beautiful promise ring, so we will be together forever. What difference does it really make? I'm not hurting anyone.* How easily I allowed my thoughts to deceive me.

Why is it, too often, only by experience do we finally understand that God's rules are for our protection and future happiness? At the time, for me, the sex had everything to do with acceptance. If I was honest with myself, I knew I was not ready and that it was wrong, but I did not listen to that voice of conscience and inner peace. We did not end up together, but rather he soon found someone else that he wanted to be with. The Holy Spirit of truth was calling out to me, but I pushed away his warning in exchange for counterfeit love. Listening would have prevented a great deal of pain and disappointment. God was helping me, wanting me to guard my thoughts. He was trying to protect me, but I did not listen.

I found myself lost in the years that followed, as I made decisions based on my own opinion and the changing views of the seventies. Going off to college led to further loss and heartbreak, like waves of a dark sea. I felt alone, and I needed the Holy Spirit to guide and comfort me, yet I was the one getting in the way of our relationship. Instead of turning to God, I closed my ears, not admitting how selfish and disobedient I had become. I hid the turmoil with good grades and a good career, looking fine on the outside but fooling myself on the inside. Now I was the one hurting people. I wanted to be loved, but I was cutting myself off from true love. I felt the pain, and I finally turned back to God. He was there for me with forgiveness and comfort. He taught me that his boundaries are for my good, and he gave me the help I needed. Nevertheless, there are lingering negative consequences of sin and wounds of the heart. I need God to help me make wise decisions—and also to heal me when I don't.

We are not very good at knowing the truth, but there is good news. Jesus's mission was to set us free from the lies that deceive us and have the potential to destroy us. The Spirit of truth is now available to everyone who calls upon God and trusts Jesus to carry away their sin. He passionately values each of us! God loves us, pursues us, comforts us, and wants to heal us with his truth and love. He is patient as we find our way; he will help us step by step as we trust him. Not only that, but he asks us to join him in his mission of truth and love. In our world, evil is the opposition, constantly trying to get us to doubt the word of God and his love for us. If we react based on lies that plant doubt and guilt, rather than the truth of God's love and God's word, we are on a dangerous course—vulnerable, insecure, and defensive. Turning to God gives us true security and helps us see more clearly. We *need* the Spirit of truth!

> The true light that gives light to everyone was coming into the world. (John 1:9)

> "If you love me, keep my commands and I will ask the Father, and he will give you another advocate to help you and be with you forever—the Spirit of truth. The world cannot accept him, because it neither sees him nor knows him. But you know him, for he lives with you and will be in you. I will not leave you as orphans; I will come to you. Before long, the world will not see me anymore, but you will see me. Because I live, you also will live. On that day you will realize that I am in my Father, and you are in me, and I am in you. Whoever has my commands and keeps them is the one who loves me. The one who loves me will be loved by my Father, and I too will love them and show myself to them." {Jesus to his followers]. (John 14:15–21)

> "When he, the Spirit of truth, comes, he will guide you into all the truth. He will not speak on his own; he will speak only what he hears, and he will tell you what is yet to come. He will glorify me because it is from me that he will receive what he will make known to you." [Jesus speaking.] (John 16:13-14)

Dear friends, since God so loved us, we ought to love one another. No one has ever seen God; but if we love one another, God lives in us and his love is made complete in us.

This is how we know that we live in him and he in us: He has given us his Spirit. And we have seen and testify that the Father has sent the Son to be the Savior of the world. If anyone acknowledges that Jesus is the Son of God, God lives in them and they in God. And so we know and rely on the love God has for us.

God is love. Whoever lives in love lives in God, and God in them. This is how love is made complete among us so that we will have confidence on the Day of Judgment: In this world we are like Jesus. (1 John 4:11–17)

Surely you desire truth in the inner parts;
    you teach me wisdom in the inmost place.
(Psalm 51:6 NIV1984)

Prayer: Father GOD, it is hard to know and acknowledge the truth. I need you! I need the Spirit of truth in order to hear and see as you do, and to act as you would. Help me acknowledge the inner struggle and then bring it to you. Heal my broken and calloused heart. I need your wisdom in the situations of my life. I want to see the people around me through your eyes. I trust Jesus to rescue me from my sin, and I ask for your Spirit to be with me. Help me!

Discussion:

1. It is easy to "bend" the truth. Have you ever thought, *I exaggerated*, or *I was not exactly truthful*, after you spoke? What motive influenced you?

2. Do you believe God knows the whole truth, and if so, do you find this scary, comforting, or both?

3. Do you believe the Spirit of truth is available to help us individually? If so, give a specific example of how he has helped you. (Conscience, Warning, Comfort, Understanding, Direction, Foreknowledge)

4. How did Jesus make our relationship with the Spirit of truth possible?

5. Read Matthew 13:1–23.
   In the explanation of the parable of the sower (verses 18–23), what things keep us from being fruitful?
   How does the Spirit of truth help us?
   Jesus said that people with healthy eyes and ears could not see or hear (verse 13). Why? See verse 15.

6. Have you ever felt the Holy Spirit of truth prompt you to make a change or do something for someone else? What happened?

CHAPTER 7

Boundary Lessons

I thought my love would be enough,
In time, all would be okay.
But the years went on and the problems grew,
Without truth, I was in the way.

Then you will understand what is right and just
  and fair—every good path.
For wisdom will enter your heart,
  and knowledge will be pleasant to your soul.
                                        —Proverbs 2:9

Truth reveals our deepest needs. It shines light on our shadows and fears. Life had taken an unexpected turn. I had found love and security with Stephen, but before long, our little church had gathered the community in remembrance, because he was gone. Two years and two moves later, on the other side of the country, we had a new life with my new husband, Michael. I did not feel as secure because his personality was introverted and often detached. God wanted me to love my new husband, so I set my mind to do it. *I can do it!* Yet without truth, relationships crumble. I was not honest with myself, let alone being honest with him. Listening to the Spirit of truth is something we learn from experience. Acknowledging the truth and keeping boundaries are an important part of the journey.

Our best effort to help a situation sometimes makes it worse. I set my mind on being a good wife for Michael and waited for results. He spent more time traveling or on his own than ever. He poured himself into his career, yet still he seemed unhappy. I learned quickly it was very hard, seemingly impossible, to open up communication about our relationship. Each time I tried, it was a disaster! Even with a counselor, attempts seemed futile, and I gave up. Before long he lived in his world, and I lived in mine. Still I attempted to show love, risked trying to do my part. Over time my efforts became shallow attempts with little feeling behind them. Instead of acknowledging my pain, I did my best to ignore it. I swept everything under the carpet and looked for happiness in my children and in pursuing endeavors that were important to me, with some success.

Thirty years went by.

This is a common story. But make no mistake, not dealing with problems only leads to bigger problems. There are areas of our lives that need to be forgiven and areas that need to be fulfilled. There are areas that need change. Hardships in our lives help bring clarity to these areas. God allowed me to suffer a chain of events (told in *Fear No Evil*, chapter 9); only then did I acknowledge how broken I was and how much pain I carried. Only then did I learn the value of inner honesty and outward boundaries.

The Mingling of Truth and Love

True love is heartfelt and sincere (Romans 12:9), and so it must be based on the truth. Otherwise, our heartfelt emotions erode. Yet true love is also a commitment, a decision that no matter what, we will demonstrate goodness to another (Romans 12:10–12, 14). There is a dynamic, spiritual aspect of love that depends on both truth and commitment. When we don't want to face the truth, or we get in the way of others experiencing the natural consequences of their actions, we in fact get in the way of true love. Healthy relationships, in which love is functioning the way it is meant to, will grow. If the love in a relationship is not growing, that is a sign that adjustments are needed. Our life on earth is all about learning to make those adjustments and learning to love more effectively. Hearts are touched and people are healed when we allow God to make the needed adjustments.

Everyone has areas in their life where love is not functioning as it should. We are born with a "me first" attitude. We feel our own wants and needs, crying out for them to be taken care of. When we're infants, it is important that our needs are attended to because it gives us the building blocks for trust. The security we have in the first years of life helps us develop healthy relationships throughout our lives. As we mature, becoming children and then adults, we learn to take into consideration the wants and needs of others. We learn the boundaries God has set in place for the welfare of mankind, and we learn to adjust our actions and reactions to consider these variables. However, we make mistakes all the time. If we double-down or give excuses and refuse to admit our mistakes (often even to ourselves), then we don't mature as we should. When we acknowledge our mistakes and turn to God for the help to improve as we go forward, we grow. Therefore, when we do not see the truth of our actions and their consequences, it stunts our growth.

Long-suffering and grace are powerful within a loving relationship, but not at the cost of truth. Love cannot thrive without accountability. Children need wise boundaries to succeed in life. Likewise, for teens and adults, overlooking bad behavior as a pattern for keeping peace just leads to future problems. Not dealing with our problems affects our growth. Denying our feelings and pain comes with building walls of protection, and the longer it goes, the higher our walls become. Inevitably the walls lead to greater problems. We need to be brave and get things out in the open, setting healthy boundaries with each other in love. There is a way through, when boundaries are enforced with consequences rather than anger and we do not allow offence and division to take root. Within this framework we grow, and grace and forgiveness can be effective to heal.

For every action, there is a reaction. Whether in physics or in life, our actions have consequences, even when we don't acknowledge their impact. For example, every spouse wants to be respected by their partner. Not showing respect is wrong. This is true for all people; we want respect, and we are in the wrong if we do not show respect to others, regardless of whether or not they have earned it. Nevertheless, if a husband or wife is unkind and demonstrates a pattern of unloving choices, their spouse may show respect, but in their heart they begin to lose it. The respect is no longer sincere, and it doesn't take long before both parties know it. Walls start to go up, because heartfelt respect based on trust is earned. If one or both resist addressing the problem, it becomes difficult to work things out. The self-worth of both is affected, and *feelings* of love begin to erode.

Communication and then the relationship break down. At this point, commitment is the glue that holds a relationship together. In marriage our commitment is a promise, sacred to God, not to be taken lightly, to love and protect through the good and the bad.

Boundaries Protect Love

Like a loving parent, God has rules for us to follow. The purpose of life's laws or boundaries is to protect people. Rules need to have consequences, so they will be effective to protect. Governments have laws with consequences and boundaries that are honored to protect the overall world community. The goal is to protect us from aggression and oppression, keeping people, communities, and nations accountable. Boundaries work best when agreed on with mutual respect. The same is true in our relationships—boundaries protect us and keep our families, and therefore our communities, healthy. As we set boundaries for how we will interact with each other, there is a choice as to whether they will be kept and enforced. Limits with consequences help us avoid putting up walls of division. When we take seriously our responsibility to enforce boundaries, with grace used in wisdom, love can grow and communities can thrive.

In the Promised Land there were boundaries (Numbers 34), never to keep peace-loving people out but rather to check aggression and give God's people a home of peace and prosperity that they could share with others. There were laws to be honored and provisions for when they weren't. This blessed nation was blessed in order to be a blessing to others (Genesis 12:2) and to demonstrate God's provision and rewards for faithfulness (Deuteronomy 5:33). There is much more to the story too—not trusting God, lots of disobedience, lots of hard times—but always God's promises prevailed.

Today, God also demonstrates his provision, as we apply the truth of God's principles. When we go outside of those boundaries by ignoring God's rules of love, things get messed up! God knows we will often fail, yet God's promises prevail. When we get things back on track with him and apply the rules of love, good comes. Setting boundaries helps us get things back on track in our relationships. If we never feel the consequences of our actions, it is unlikely we will change and trust God. Instead, we will just keep doing what we are doing, trying to control the situation for our benefit. Through the process of coming up against boundaries, we are forced to face our harmful attitudes and actions, as well as how we are ultimately hurting ourselves.

Many factors come into play—the patterns we grow up with, our cultural and political attitudes, our economic situation, our mental health, etc. Establishing healthy boundaries helps us face each of these factors and begin to learn how they are affecting our relationships. They give us the framework of protection needed for people to heal and for relationships to grow. If there are no honored boundaries, walls of division will begin to block the road to love. Rather than loving homes and community, walls of separation and hate pop up. We are all going to make mistakes, so it is wise to overlook something that happens which is out of character. Communication as to why something uncharacteristic happens helps us understand each other's stress and difficulties. However, when there is a pattern of crossing healthy boundaries, consequences must be put in place and enforced. You are not doing anyone a favor by allowing them to demonstrate a *pattern* of crossing healthy boundaries.

General Relational Boundaries:

- Being truthful about facts
- Being truthful about feelings, expressing them gracefully
- Being willing to listen and consider others' feelings and how they perceive the truth
- Being treated and treating others with respect
- Not allowing offence to take root in our minds
- No name-calling or violence
- No sexual abuse or adultery
- No substance abuse
- Doing our work
- Doing our best to live within our economic situation
- No cheating or stealing
- Seeking to honor God and family in our choices and actions

It's not easy to keep boundaries and submit to appropriate consequences when they are crossed. Even agreeing on what would constitute breaking each boundary can be challenging. Yet with the help of God and others (family, friends, a faith community, and trusted counselors), we need to take the challenge seriously. If we pray for each other and seek God's help in choosing and maintaining boundaries, he will help us. Sometimes love means being mature and humble enough to submit to the rules of engagement and tough enough to hold accountable those you care about. Try to steer clear from using words of accusation, but rather do your best to choose words that seek mutual understanding. Don't let someone who disregards boundaries claim you are their problem. Do your part, follow through in keeping boundaries, give it time, forgive, and commit to love through it all. The rest is their choice. God is looking for you to do your part with his help (Romans 12:17–18), and sometimes that means taking a hard road.

In the case of families there is a lot to balance as we consider how boundaries are enforced. Keeping families together is a priority. However, there are also times when a spouse or children are in jeopardy and then separation becomes necessary. Absolutely seek out help and refuge if there is a patterns of abuse or violence in your home. Physical safety is a must. Be careful not to let emotions rule. Step back to consider the big picture, yet don't back away from working on the problems. The goal is that each member of the family feels loved and safe. To find fulfilment, we cannot jump relational boundaries. Seek forgiveness and make amends when you do. Value yourself enough to enforce the boundaries of protection and love. It doesn't help anyone when you don't. Look for the help you need. Healthy families are not possible without committing to do the work.

Michael and I are no longer hiding or running away from our relationship. God is teaching us to be vulnerable and honest about our feelings, after a long time of trying to ignore them. Real hope is born out of truth, not hiding from it. Both hardships and boundaries woke us up to the truth and uncovered the buried problems. They helped us to understand where we need to change and ask God for help. Some say people don't change, but God makes it clear that he believes we can—we must! Sometimes change takes a long time, but God does not give up on us. It's easy to fall back into familiar unhealthy patterns, yet with God's help and open communication we can change and heal. Praying together helps to keep us compassionate, open, and willing. I have renewed hope for a strong marriage, and now, we are on the road to get there.

I've come to realize that God knows us better than we know ourselves. He knows our secrets and our deepest needs. God loves us as we are but cares enough to move us toward a better place. He wants everyone to have a loving home—a place to feel secure and valued. Some families embrace God's guidelines, and their love grows. But for many, a loving home is not their reality, and let's be honest, here on earth no home is perfect. With hope, we can look forward to our heavenly home. Life on earth is designed to get us there.

Prepared for the Pearl Gates

In the book of Revelation, John described his vision of heaven. He saw the new "promised land," where the pearl gates were never closed, a Holy City, beautifully prepared as a bride for her husband. "It shone with the glory of God, and its brilliance was like that of a very precious jewel, like a jasper, clear as crystal" (Revelation 21:11). But the thing is, by definition jasper is opaque because of all the impurities or sediments mixed within. Jasper can be any color and is formed under pressure, but light cannot pass through it. And so John sees a miracle—a stone like jasper, but as clear as crystal. The impurities no longer blocking the light, it becomes pure crystal—symbolic of the miracle of us presented pure—by trusting in Jesus.

The foundation of the Holy City is made up of beautiful, precious gemstones, also formed under pressure. The pressures of life are often the catalyst for our trust and purification. Working through life's difficulties plays an important role in bringing about the change we need to mature. Overcoming the challenges of life helps us grow and become more loving. Through our relationship with God, trusting his love and obeying his word, we build a beautiful, strong foundation that can carry us through the storms of life. Whether John's vision of heaven is only symbolic or also physical, we do not know for sure, but we do know this: "Nothing impure will ever enter it, nor will anyone who does what is shameful or deceitful, but only those whose names are written in the Lamb's book of life" (Revelation 21:27). Jesus, the Lamb of God, came to cover our sin, shame, and deceit—a miracle, sinful men and women seen as pure (clear as crystal), enrolled in the Lamb's book of life. Men and women who trust God are purified in the pressures of life, step by step, as they are vulnerable enough to allow the Spirit of truth to make the needed adjustments. God values truth. Don't get in the way of letting the light pass through.

> "My son, do not make light of the Lord's discipline,
>   and do not lose heart when he rebukes you,
> because the Lord disciplines the ones he loves,
>   and he chastens everyone he accepts as his son."

> Endure hardship as discipline; God is treating you as his children. For what children are not disciplined by their father? ... God disciplines us for our good, in order that we may share in his holiness. No discipline seems pleasant at the time, but painful. Later on, however it produces a harvest of righteousness and peace for those who have been trained by it. (Hebrews 12:5–7, 10–11)

My life has been a journey of learning to love. Along the way, God has taught me patience and grace. He has taught me to look to him for my worth and love. I've learned what it really means to be "tough" when it is called for—not by a stoic denial of my feelings, but rather by valuing my feelings and seeking to understand their greater purpose. Our good will and actions matter, but do not alone change hearts, especially when the truth is not dealt with. *God* works within us to change our hearts, grace and truth both playing an important role. Sometimes it's through boundaries and hardships that we finally own-up and deal with the truth. It's then that true love has a chance.

In heaven, truth and love mingle in perfect harmony. Our life journeys are designed to prepare us for our eternal destiny. I want to be ready to go home. God's hope is that we all embrace his gift. Will our names be written in the Lamb's book of life; will we be part of God's family? To be prepared, we can't skip the hard stuff, but thankfully, happiness and hope are also a part of our journeys. God gives us the blessings of love and laughter and fun. He wants us to discover our passions and purposes, making a difference for others. And I can hardly wait to tell you about my adventures!

> The LORD is compassionate and gracious,
>> slow to anger, abounding in love.
> He will not always accuse,
>> nor will he harbor his anger forever;
> he does not treat us as our sins deserve
>> or repay us according to our iniquities.
> For as high as the heavens are above the earth,
>> so great is his love for those who fear him;
> as far as the east is from the west,
>> so far has he removed our transgressions from us.
> (Psalm 103:8-12)

Today I have given you the choice between life and death, between blessings and curses. Now I call on heaven and earth to witness the choice you make. Oh, that you would choose life, so that you and your descendants might live! You can make this choice by loving the Lord your God, obeying him, and committing yourself firmly to him. This is the key to life.(Deuteronomy 30:19–20a NLT)

> The boundary lines have fallen for me in pleasant places;
>> surely I have a delightful inheritance.
> I will praise the Lord, who counsels me;
>> even at night my heart instructs me.
> I keep my eyes always on the Lord.
>> With him at my right hand, I will not be shaken.
>> (Psalm 16:6–8)

Discussion:

1. Do you find it easy or difficult to set and keep boundaries?
2. How do you react to the boundaries or rules of others?
3. Do you trust that the boundaries and rules of God are for your benefit?
4. As you look back, can you see how God has used any boundaries set in your life (by God or by others) to help you grow?
5. Read Matthew 7:24–27, the Parable of the Wise and Foolish Builder. Why is putting God's word of truth into practice important?
6. What are some boundaries that are necessary for good relationships?
7. How can seeking truth and having boundaries help us adjust our lives to God's loving direction?

CHAPTER 8

Passion with Purpose

I took a step of love today,
Though part of me said no.
I struggled to take this first small step,
But God helped my love to show.

Looking to Jesus with each new step,
Within me, my passion grew.
I found the life God planned for me,
And the joy of life renewed!

"The thief comes only in order to steal, kill, and destroy.
I have come in order that you might have life—life in all
its fullness."

—John 10:10 (GNB)

"Life in all its fullness" is a satisfying life of contentment and purpose. It is an active live, in which we find rest for our souls. God created us, each with our own personality, interests, and abilities. He had in mind what we each would do (Ephesians 2:10). Each of us has a purpose—specific tasks, vocations, callings, and relationships—envisioned by God to accomplish his good plan. God weaves our lives together to bring about *his* will, while taking into account our freewill. When we immerse ourselves in God's love—trusting him with our relationships, stress, and pain—we emerge to take our part in his dynamic plan. Our dreams evolve to become part of God's overall mission of love.

"I like being here," Yusuf said with a heavy accent. "Working all day, it's good to relax and have some fun." He was one of the thousands of international students employed in the coastal city each summer as a crucial part of the workforce. Yusuf had found this special niche—a place to play music, join games, enjoy food, and learn some conversational English, all for free. The international coffee house provided a place to slow down, relax, and experience God's love.

Students from all over the world gather here to learn about each other. It's even a place where students from rival countries can become good friends! It was all Mark's vision, his passion realized. Soon after Mark graduated from university in civil engineering, God called him and his wife Ana to full-time ministry. Their first years, they served in Africa. He was working within his profession, as a water engineer. As time went on, their love for future generations became their full-time passion. Mark has a God-given spark that draws young people and a gift for teaching. Ana is like a mom to students. Eventually, they focused in on serving international students, who appreciate their support, being far from their home and culture. They both understand what that's like.

I met them as the dream emerged.

Mark was asked to speak at the city prayer breakfast. I had never gone, but the year he was to speak, I had the repeated thought to attend. I stopped at my church to get a ticket, but they were sold out. *That's okay, I didn't want to travel into the city that early anyway.* I headed down the highway, putting it out of my mind. But then I saw the place the secretary had mentioned; a business that might still have tickets. *Here I go.* I held my breath as I swerved into the parking lot. Sure enough, I had a ticket!

The previous summer, I had tried to connect with international students in the coastal city but was not very successful. I had organized a few free lunch events; not well attended. Meanwhile, Mark had a vision for the coffeehouse, providing regular nights of fun and language learning as well as cultural activities. At the city prayer breakfast, he shared his dream. Afterward, I gave my name and number to his wife, doubtful I would actually hear from them (you know how it goes). A month later I received a call. They lived four hours away and were coming to town. The three of us met at my kitchen table to plan and pray.

Mark followed through with his God-given vision, and God brought me and many others alongside to help make it a reality. The local churches were providing free meals and welcomed Mark and Ana to join them, providing a great opportunity to meet the international students. Volunteers from several of the countries represented come each summer to help as well. Through the years, the coffeehouse has been a great success. It makes for long hours, from breakfast with students to the midnight drive home, but Mark loves his work. We all enjoy the students, and they naturally experience God's love.

The God who created this world, who knows the past, present, and future, has a place and role in mind for each of us. God's all-encompassing plan weaves the lives of people together throughout history. Men and women are looking for significance and meaning and are designed this way for a purpose. We can discover our place in God's dynamic plan, as we develop our gifts and passions. God already knows the decisions we will make, and uses our choices to draw us and guide us. (Many scholars believe time in eternity cannot be measured in the linear increments known to us on earth.) God knows the future, and he knows us (much better than we know ourselves). He knows the choices we will make, and they factor into his plan. We learn from our bad decisions, as well as the good.

Finding our purpose starts with small steps of love. Sometimes we don't feel like taking a step, but we make a choice to do it anyway. God delights in those decisions in our lives, developing our character through them. As we respond to God, our hearts soften, and we become more thankful and aware of his love. Often our feelings will follow our obedience, and from there, God will cultivate a passion within us. Our purpose in life will be discovered and fueled by our God-given passions, which develop as we interact with him and each other. Our passions and purpose motivate us to go forward and give us the strength to persevere.

The predominant meaning of the word *passion* has evolved in a fascinating sequence. The origin of the English word *passion* (from late Latin *passio*, "suffering") is reflected in the primary definition: "the sufferings of Jesus Christ between the night of the Last Supper and his death." Merriam-Webster's Dictionary lists a second, meaning, SUFFERING (definition 2), noting it as obsolete. The third meaning, "the state or capacity of being acted on by external agents or forces" (def. 3) we will consider further. And finally, Webster lists EMOTION (def. 4a), and LOVE (def. 5a), both listing submeanings with positive and negative connotations (merriam-webster.com).

Urban Dictionary's top contemporary definition states beautifully: "Passion is when you put more energy into something than is required to do it. It is more than just enthusiasm or excitement, passion is ambition that is materialized into action to put as much heart, mind, body and soul into something as possible" (urbandictionary.com). The progression of the meaning of the word *passion* mirrors the progression of developing healthy and meaningful passion within our lives. As childlike idealism fades and we grasp for meaning in life, our realization of *Jesus's passion for us, demonstrated on the cross*, gives us new hope and renders *eternal suffering "obsolete"* for all who follow him. As we allow the Spirit of truth into our lives, we can win *the battle that will come from external forces* that want to steal our passions with counterfeit love. We find God-given purpose and fulfillment as we learn to *love, demonstrated by action that we can put our heart, mind, body, and soul into.*

We could summarize the meaning of *passion* as "intense emotion or purpose compelling us to action." We will never see a more intense emotion of love leading to any greater action of love than Jesus going to the cross for his creation! The book of Hebrews gives us a clue to Jesus's motivation—"He endured the cross, ignoring the shame, for the sake of the *joy* that was laid out in front of him, and sat down at the right side of God's throne" (Hebrews 12:2 CEB, italics added). Jesus is overjoyed that the ultimate power of death is now defeated for *everyone* who turns to him (Romans 8)!

The deceiving evil one, who manipulates the truth, tries to trick us into thinking God wants us to suffer as he suffered, rather than the truth that *he was willing to suffer in our place.* God loves us and wants the best for us. He wants us to have *true* happiness—joy. He cries with us in our sorrow (John 11:35). We suffer in this world because evil is present among us. God allows it, knowing that through trial our character grows, preparing us for our future.

Sometimes, evil and free will come together with terrifying results, but be assured: God carries the sorrows and souls of the innocent and will bring judgment on those who pursue evil. Other times, we choose to suffer for the sake of others. God is not pleased to see us suffer, but he approves of our willing sacrifices for the good of others. He wants us to have life to the fullest, a meaningful life! On the cross, God won the battle that raged between good and evil, so he could be present with us in the battle between good and evil that vies for our passions. His passion is us!

The battle between good and evil is active in influencing the passions we develop, and it is important that we are aware. The third meaning listed in Webster's—"being acted upon by external agents or forces"—is something we have all experienced. For example, if a husband or wife has a passionate relationship with their spouse, it is a wonderful and good gift from God. However, if one develops a passion for someone outside their marriage, there may be an *external agent*, or evil influence, at work trying to destroy their lives. A passion for our job is very positive, yet if that passion derails us from our family or God's plan, it has a negative impact. We can develop a passion that is healthy or a passion that is harmful. A passion can be motivated by greed or motivated by caring for others. Our own desires, combined with temptations from outside influences or *forces*, can affect what passions we develop. Is it lust or pure love? Is it arrogance or compassion? The battle between good and evil influences what we pursue.

When we begin to feel passion arise, we should ask ourselves: *What is its source? Is it from the Spirit of truth, or am I being drawn away from God?* Our thoughts generate our feelings, which influence our passions—not the other way around, as most people think. Since our feelings usually develop from our thoughts, we need to guard them! As thoughts and ideas cross our minds, we need to consider whether they are ours alone, from an evil source, or from God. Discard quickly thoughts that are impure, violent, unkind or that take offense. These types of thoughts are *never* from God. They steal from our lives and, given opportunity to take root, can ultimately destroy us.

To have the power to guard our minds, it's important to have a relationship with our living God, talking to him each day, reading and reflecting on his word—aligning ourselves with him. We can replace harmful thoughts by memorizing some of our favorite Bible verses. Our lives and relationships improve when we dwell on true and positive thoughts. "Whatever is true, whatever is noble, whatever is right, whatever is pure, whatever is lovely, whatever is admirable—if anything is excellent or praiseworthy—think about such things" (Philippians 4:8). Focusing on the good around us, the blessings and bright spots, makes us more attractive to others. We project a healthy positive vibe.

When we rely on the Spirit of truth to guard our thoughts, he begins to stir healthy passions within us. God made us and knows what roles we will be passionate about. As we respond to his direction, our passions develop. This is the key to living a meaningful life—a life full of purpose. The Holy Spirit of truth wants to fuel our passions, motivating us to action, that will touch the lives of others. Our active response allows us to grow in maturity and discover God's will for our lives, ultimately bringing us joy!

Our passions often develop in areas that will use our natural and spiritual gifts. Natural gifts are talents we are born with, though they still require our time and effort to develop. We have a choice whether to cultivate them and whether to use them for good. Some examples are a beautiful voice, a mechanical ability, a gifted way with children, or a mind for business.

Spiritual gifts are given by God to his followers. These added gifts are used to encourage each other, and to help men, women, and children discover the reality of God for themselves. Spiritual gifts are developed as we use them in faith, such as wisdom, teaching, and healing (1 Corinthians 12). A positive change in our character, transforming us into a person of depth and beauty, is also part of our spiritual gifting. "The fruit of the Spirit is love, joy, peace, forbearance, kindness, goodness, faithfulness, gentleness and self-control" (Galatians 5:22–23). Often our natural and spiritual gifts work together to accomplish our God-given purpose, and our passion fuels our efforts as we take steps forward to develop them.

The gifts we are given in life, whether natural, spiritual, or material, grow as we use them to enhance the lives of others. This is one of God's basic principles. The Parable of the Talents, recorded in Matthew 25:14–30, (talents refer to valuable coins in the parable) teaches that God entrusts even more to those who are faithful to *use* their resources, gifts, and abilities "It is required that those who have been given a trust must prove faithful" (1 Corinthians 4:2).

God's plan is interactive. He has placed each of us in a place of community and a time of history, with the talents, gifts, and passion needed to accomplish his will. Yet we have a choice: to participate or not. When we take action, we learn, we grow, and we are entrusted with more. Sometimes we discover our purpose early and are drawn to a vocation, trade, or profession suited to us. Family can be our passion—parenting and providing stability for others to grow or fulfill their purpose. We may have a calling to a particular group of people or cause. God may give us a particular task or mission to complete. Our passions and purpose often change throughout the seasons of our lives. Just seeking to stay in God's will, we can't help but make a difference; your loving attitude and presence will play a role in his plan. It is never too late to seek God for your purpose and find fulfilment.

In a family or community, we each have different gifts. Together we accomplish what no one could alone, and as a result, we find the connection we are looking for. Churches can meet a variety of needs within a community, each having their own area of service. Families participate and grow in their love for each other. Communities thrive as God's people work in cooperation with local government and other organizations. Reflecting God's character naturally helps others develop and renew faith. They see evidence of God's presence and care. Families and communities start to feel secure. God weaves our lives together, and our vision expands.

It's a Small World

As I look back, I can see God has placed me in places and situations that have, in turn, given my life purpose. I developed passions that I never dreamed I would have. At one point, a move we made landed us in an exceptionally missions-minded church. It changed the way I thought about our world and led to having missionaries live in our home from time to time. When my children were in elementary school, we all traveled to China and Indonesia to visit missionaries—a trip that influenced our worldview in a positive way. A few years later two talented young women, one Turkish (Asya) and one Egyptian-American, lived with our family for a year. My volunteer work with international students strengthened my passion for the peoples of the world. All of these experiences influenced the course of my life.

A miracle day in the summer of 2012 fueled my passion for the country of Turkey; a passion that I had no idea I would develop. Stay with me as I set the stage; it's a bit hard to follow, but the story is amazing. During the spring I had traveled to Kazakhstan to visit some students while I was on my way to China. We had become friends while they were working summer jobs in the USA. While in Kazakhstan, I met another young woman named Libby. She had been healed of fourth-stage Hodgkin's lymphoma, living a year with a family in Turkey for treatment. The following summer Libby came to the USA for a few months as a volunteer at the international coffeehouse.

Just after Libby left to return to Kazakhstan, Asya (the young Turkish woman who had lived with our family and was now a flight attendant) offered me a free trip with her to Istanbul. Asya had always wanted me to visit her beautiful, hospitable country. Within a week I was on the plane, excited about the opportunity to spend time with her and experience Istanbul. (Like many Americans, I had many misconceptions about Turkey.) A few days after we arrived, Asya was unexpectedly called to cover another flight but hoped to return soon. I was on my own. How I wished I had the contact information for the family that Libby had stayed with; she had told me they spoke English and were from the States. Nevertheless, I was content to have God as my companion as I explored Istanbul or sat by the hotel pool.

I was reading *The Circle Maker* by Mark Batterson. As I read, I had the feeling (a strong repeated thought) that God was asking me to circle the country of Turkey in prayer. *Well, of course I'm having that thought; I'm reading* The Circle Maker! *God, are you really asking me to pray around Turkey, or is this one of my own crazy ideas? Please help me to know if you really want me to do it.* I went through the rest of the week without any confirmation of whether this thought was from God or my own, and yet the thought was not dimming.

The day of confirmation.

It was Sunday, my last full day in Istanbul. I decided to go to an international church I had found online, located just off Istiklal Street in Taskim. It was on a long touristic street in another part of the city, but I didn't have the exact address. I took the hotel shuttle bus to Taskim. Arriving, I was relieved to see a building with a cross atop it. I thought it must be the church and entered, not realizing it was the French consulate. The disgruntled guard stopped me and sent me on my way. I started down Istiklal Street, asking several people, but no one could tell me where the church was, if they could understand me at all. With each passing block I became more discouraged, not knowing, literally or figuratively, where I was, or where I was going. I began to pray silently, telling God how discouraged I felt, how I needed some kind of confirmation. *How can I return to travel around all of Turkey, when I can't even find this church?* I asked God to help me and told him how I needed him to direct my life. Just then, I heard English voices from a couple walking beside me, so I asked if they happened to know where the church was. To my surprise, they told me they had gone to an earlier service and would be happy to show me the way! As we introduced ourselves, I told them where I was from.

"We know a young woman who traveled to that city as a volunteer this past summer," they said.

"Libby!" I exclaimed, wondering if it could be.

They looked at me in amazement. It was true. They were the couple who had taken care of her! *There are almost twenty million people in Istanbul, yet I happen to meet this couple randomly on the street!*

I had a strong sense of God's presence with me at church. The message was about how great, how deep, and how amazing God's love is for each of us and for all people. After church everyone was invited for lunch in a courtyard nearby. I met a young woman there and shared what had happened; how I met the couple who had cared for Libby. I also mentioned the name of another man (a friend of a friend) whom I had hoped to meet, but he lived on the Asian side of Istanbul. I had unsuccessfully tried to contact him, hoping to travel to the Asian side and meet his family. She looked at me wide-eyed; he was coming in just a few minutes to pick her up! Though it had been a sunny day, it began to rain and hail just as he arrived. We had some time to talk in the covered courtyard. As the weather cleared and the sun returned, we left, and I made my way back to the shuttle bus just in time.

On the ride back I hoped to take a picture at a particular spot that reflected the vast amount of people who live in Istanbul; no particular landmark. At that spot the driver pulled over and stopped, without my asking! He motioned for me to get out, indicating in broken English that he would wait. *That was unlikely.* We returned to the hotel, and just as I entered, the storm came up again with great power—wind, rain, and hail. What a remarkable morning! I knew it had been orchestrated by God, and it gave me confidence that he *was* directing me. I wrote down everything that had happened and then decided the day was not over.

The sun was shining again. I still had time to look for Saint Stephen's Church, which I wanted to see in honor of my late husband, Stephen. I had heard of a big cathedral with that name that was worth seeing. Earlier in the week I had tried to find it without success, but a Turkish man had given me an address on a piece of paper. It was not too far from my hotel, so I got a taxi. The driver weaved in and out of narrow streets and stopped at a tall double door, along a stone wall, that was cracked open.

I entered the courtyard to see this was not a big cathedral at all but a modest and charming chapel. Peeking inside, I saw a man standing at an open window in the courtyard. He had a basket of candles and offered me one before directing me to the entrance. I went forward to pray, alone in the small chapel. The light flowed in through the stained-glass windows.

When I finished, I arose to see a woman standing at the back, perfectly centered in the aisle, with the light streaming in behind her. The vision of her stayed in my mind for years. She had dark bobbed hair, wore a flared skirt, and held a basket of grapes. She asked me if I would like to light my candle and showed me how. She spoke English and explained to me that this was not the only Saint Stephen's church in the town. There were three, and yet none of them was the famous cathedral. Actually, the town itself had been named Saint Stephen at one time, she explained as she guided me, pointing out the location of each church. Then, she left to meet her mother for tea, telling me I could walk along the sea to get back to my hotel.

I explored each church and then started back, enjoying the colorful fishing boats, the crisp air, and the pastel clouds billowing over the sea. The backdrop of deep blue sky made the light and colors vibrant after the storm. As I walked, full of joy, I heard the woman whom I had met at Saint Stephen's call out to me, "Hello!" She had spotted me and asked if I would join them for tea. It was lovely. Three months later I returned to circle Turkey in prayer—a trip I will never forget. God gave me the gift of an amazing day and a new passion for Turkey!

God's word tells us that when he created each of us, he had in mind our role (Ephesians 2:10). Our personalities, abilities, gifts, and decisions all interact to become part of God's plan. He has made each of us unique and placed us within a time, community, and world to touch the lives of others in our own way. As we discover our God-given purposes in our family, community, work, or life mission, we take our part in God's overall plan for humanity. Though each of us is unique, we are also quite similar, sharing the same basic needs—for love, acceptance, provision, protection, and purpose. God calls us to be his ambassadors—his light in the darkness, guiding and helping people to meet these needs. The Spirit in us enables us to love others and be active in their lives. Acts of our care become stepping-stones in the path for others, guiding *their* journey to know God's love and purposes for their lives. Our personal faith grows and hope rises for others, as they experience our spark of kindness, fight for justice, or the blessings brought with prayer. With passion, he has chosen *us* to reveal his love to the world!

> I know the plans I have in mind for you, declares the Lord; They are plans for peace, not disaster, to give you a future filled with hope. When you call me and come and pray to me, I will listen to you. When you search for me, yes, search for me with all of your heart, you will find me. (Jeremiah 29:11-13 CEB)

> We are therefore Christ's ambassadors, as though God were making his appeal through us. (2 Corinthians 5:20)

We are God's handiwork, created in Christ Jesus to do good works, which God prepared in advance for us to do. (Ephesians 2:10)

You are the light of the world .... Let your light shine before others, that they may see your good deeds and glorify your Father in heaven. (Matthew 5:14, 16)

Many, Lord my God,
 are the wonders you have done,
 the things you planned for us.
None can compare with you;
 were I to speak and tell of your deeds,
 they would be too many to declare. ...
I desire to do your will, my God;
 your law is within my heart." (Psalm 40:5, 8)

Discussion:

1. It is common to hesitate or talk ourselves out of taking a step of love. What stops us?
2. Have you ever obeyed God in a small thing that led to knowing more about the plan God had for your life? Explain.
3. Why is it important to consider the source of passions that develop within us?
4. Are certain activities or influences robbing from you a life of purpose and contentment? What steps could you take to pursue your relationship with God and to live a life of purpose?
5. Is there anything you are passionate about—an interest, cause, career, or concern for someone?
   Do you know anyone else with a similar or related interest?
6. What do you think your talents or gifts are? What do others say they are?
7. Have you ever experienced a time when you felt God was leading you to do something? What happened?

CHAPTER 9
Fear No Evil

Wonderful, our world was created,
We were happy, knowing love at the start.
Then evil seduced our free will,
Beginning the battle for hearts.

Now we're searching for purpose and meaning,
And we try to make sense of the fight.
More than a test, it's our pathway,
To find what is true and is right.

Malice and Majesty opposing,
Battling for minds and for souls.
Humbly we realize we're helpless,
Until God is given control.

God's promise: to stand beside us,
Seeing us through the storm.
We have a part in the battle,
But He's already won the war.

"Do not be afraid."
—The words of Jesus in Matthew 10:26, 28; 28:10,
Luke 12:4, 7, 32; John 12:15; 14:27; Acts 18:9

Action hero adventures, the classic Disney movies, and our favorite fairy tales all have one thing in common—the battle between good and evil. Often these stories suggest a spiritual aspect to the battle, something happening beyond what we can see. They depict an evil entity or villain with a dominating influence, actively seeking to deceive the goodness or innocence of the hero or heroine.

Is there a cosmic battle taking place between darkness and light? If we take an honest look at the world, our nightly world news, or our local headlines, it's there—a fight between good and evil that seems to defy logic. Think back in your own life. Have you ever made a bad decision based on deception? Don't get me wrong. We can make plenty on our own, for our own selfish reasons, but sometimes outside influences come into play. We believe a lie that plays on our vulnerability or weakness, and we are pulled in a direction we thought we would never go. Then we begin to justify our attitudes and actions, not wanting to face our part or our guilt, and before long our hearts get a little harder. Now evil has the upper hand, and we begin to believe wrong is right.

The influence of evil is everywhere. It's both subtle and bold. Evil's aim is to keep mankind separated from God. He tells us that we don't need God, that God doesn't care, God's rules are stupid, we're not good enough, that God's not real! The lies go on and on, and we struggle to know what's true. We are vulnerable to evil's lies.

Our susceptibility is extremely serious. There are times a life is so vulnerable that hopelessness, pain, or thoughts of guilt even lead to suicide. Despair that deep, brought by the lies of the evil one, is heart wrenching. God longs to redeem our sorrow and despair. He longs to forgive and heal us. Even in the darkest night or situation, there is hope; God loves each of us deeply and longs to give rest to our souls. God covers the vulnerable heart.

The effects of evil in our world should not be taken lightly. From natural evil (such as storms, sickness, and death) to sinister evil (where a choice to harm is made), the effects are beyond our comprehension. Look into the eyes of a mother or father who has lost a child; nothing will ever be the same. One more person slain in the unending fight for justice brings tears to our eyes. Jesus, too, wept at death. He healed the sick and raised the dead. He understood far more than we ever will, as his life purpose centered around saving us from evil and redeeming the sorrow and pain. Jesus explained. "The thief's [evil one's] purpose is to steal and kill and destroy. My purpose is to give them a rich and satisfying life. I am the good shepherd. The good shepherd sacrifices his life for the sheep" (John 10:10–11 NLT).

The influences and effects of evil in our world must be opposed, and we are called to be active in the fight. God's interactive plan includes us! Jesus covers and calls us. When we become his brothers and sisters, it comes with the responsibility to oppose evil and help protect the vulnerable. Our response is our path to a purposeful life. We each have a part in his plan to overcome evil. Jesus gives us focus. He tells us not to be afraid of what can kill the body, but rather beware of what can destroy our souls (Matthew 10:28). When we are on his side, the winning side, our eternal life is secure. Don't underestimate what our lives contribute, one way or the other, to the struggle and the outcome of the ongoing war between good and evil. We are called to make an impact against evil, as we guard our hearts with God's love. We have a role to play in our homes, communities, and sometimes even in another part of the world. Just as in our favorite stories, love shows up in the midst of the battle and wins in the end—in the light of eternity. The battle may intensify, but God is with us! History is full of stories of the battle between good and evil—many more inspiring than mine. Still, I will share one that I experienced, as it ends with such an amazing, yet true, story of assurance.

My battle intensified in a series of difficult, life-altering events. It was becoming hard to walk, hard to travel for English clubs, and hard to care for my grandchildren. Because of a slight structural abnormality at birth, orthopedic surgeries have been a part of my life. At that time, ankle reconstruction was needed in order for me to continue walking. I was told a week off my feet was the expected recovery time, but after a week, the surgeon instructed me not to take a step for at least four more months. Nine months later, it needed to be redone.

In the meantime, a large lump was growing in my neck. It was misdiagnosed as nothing serious, but it continued to grow. The doctors suggested having it removed because of the size—my choice, no hurry. It took a skilled surgeon over three hours to pry it from my carotid artery.

(Was evil going for my jugular?) A biopsy revealed a big surprise—I had stage four throat cancer. I had never smoked but had the marker for the HPV virus. There was much I wanted accomplish, but instead I needed to leave my home for chemotherapy and radiation treatment. Before long I was not even able to drive. Though my husband was there for the diagnosis, even sensing it was coming, he seemed to withdraw all the more as I faced the difficult year ahead. I could no longer care for my grandchildren while my youngest daughter was at university, so he helped there. Turmoil abounded. My sister Jeanne stepped in and carried a heavy load, taking a leave from teaching at one point. My oldest daughter had a newborn and had just returned to work from her maternity leave, so my son took a leave of absence and traveled cross-country to take a turn caring for me. I remember how he tried to lift my spirit, driving me through the park after treatment each day, on the way back to our rented rooms.

Even after returning home, I lay in bed for months, barely able to smile. I would look out the window, hoping for a bird to fly by, to bring me a moment of happiness. As the months passed, shock would register on visitors' faces, not sure I would make it through. I had lost my hair and fifty pounds—now just skin and bones. My sister begged me to fight harder and force myself to get out of bed!

Amazingly, over one hundred cards came for me that year, becoming a symbol of God's faithfulness. I was assured that people were praying for me. God was gracious! The doctors were wonderful, and the treatment had advanced over the years. The best medical care and *countless* people's prayers had seen me through. The chemotherapy took a good deal of my hearing and thirty-four radiation treatments left me with a tender mouth, but I was alive! And thin.

As we began to breathe a sigh of relief, my youngest sister, Jenny, discovered she had lung cancer. Just as I was rising from my own bed, I went to her. I wanted to give her hope. She died two months later, just before Christmas. Jenny was gone, leaving her three young adult children without a parent (their father had died years before). She was also the one who had looked out for my dad, who lived alone on his farm nearby. Two months later he became ill, and we brought him down to live in my home. As I recovered my strength, I cared for him, as he had dementia and cancer. Just short of two years later, he also died. A couple of weeks before he died, in misery, he said, "It's not that bad. You do what you have to do," the mantra of his life.

Meanwhile, my marriage fell apart, and my husband left. Problems that might have never been addressed surfaced during these difficult days. We could no longer sweep them under the rug without tripping over them. My husband Michael had withdrawn throughout our marriage, so I might have seen it coming, but honestly, I didn't. My daughter had graduated, so she and her children had already moved into their own home. Then Dad died, and I was alone. Thankfully, the following summer the house was full again, as the international team made use of my empty rooms. For three years, I waited with hope for my marriage.

Some would say I was cursed with such a line of unfortunate events. I knew in my heart that was not true; God was there, as a friend I could talk to and a loving Father. He had seen me through. Yet the result of sin naturally brings calamity, so I asked God if there was unrecognized sin that continued in my life, contributing to so much hardship. No one yet loves freely and my desire was for him to search and heal my heart. God went out of his way to assure me, with his love and acceptance. That spring, God touched my life with hope, in a miraculous and personal way—wonderful happenings, flashes of the proof of love!

I felt compelled to return to Istanbul after fighting for my life, losing my sister, and seeing my marriage dissolving after thirty years. A memory kept returning—the woman holding the basket of grapes in the small chapel, the light streaming in behind her. *Maybe I need to go back there to find the purpose of my life*; a typical self-focused thought. But the more I thought about it, maybe it was not about me at all, but about the people of that church.

There are over twenty million people in Istanbul and God loves every one of them. The Muslim people, just like many of us, are trying to earn God's approval, earn their way to heaven. They are hoping their good deeds will outweigh their bad. That is a burden no one can carry. I thought, *This little church is there, and they all speak Turkish. Could they (or do they) play an important role in telling the message of good news—the message of forgiveness and hope found in Jesus?* I wondered how active the church was and what they believed. I could go there to learn and pray. My family supported my plan to get away for ten days, and I knew this was where I should go.

Just as the tulip festival was to begin in Istanbul, I booked a ticket on Turkish Airlines and a room on Airbnb. I had always wanted to see the tulips, so if I was going back, why not then? Only later did I realize I had booked the ticket for Easter weekend. *Oh no. I really look forward to Easter dinner and an Easter egg hunt in our yard.* My ticket was nonrefundable, so we celebrated early. On Palm Sunday my family gathered for Easter festivities, and I took an overnight flight the following Thursday.

The taxi weaved through the cobblestone streets along the Marmara Sea. I had chosen a room in the home of a local couple who lived in the same part of the city as the church. The apartment was on the top floor, and I pulled my suitcase up the spiral marble staircase, the cats greeting me along the way. My host had both a bright personality and appearance. I was very lucky, in that she spoke English, her third language. She welcomed me, making me feel at ease. Once I was settled in, I was anxious to see how far I was from the little chapel that I had come to pray in each day—blocks, miles. Would I need a taxi? My host, Aza, said she was going out and she would show me the way. We went about a block and came to a stone church, but it was not the church I was looking for. We went several more blocks and came to a larger cathedral.

"No, this is not it, it's a smaller church with a courtyard and school nearby," I said.

"I have to go, but I think you will find it up that alleyway," she replied, as she pointed back, but to an alley just a bit higher. All three churches had the same root name, Saint Stephen. Taking the narrow cobblestone road that branched back in the direction we had come from, I found the familiar double doors that led to the courtyard. The last time I'd come, I was the only person in the chapel, until the woman with the basket of grapes appeared. Entering the courtyard, I was quite surprised—there were so many people I could not even enter in the chapel sanctuary! Jet-lagged, I had not realized it was Good Friday.

To my delight, I had come just in time for a candlelight service. In my mind I heard, *Enter in,* more than once, so I thought, *This is not a time to hesitate—do it!* I squeezed through the crowd just as the candles were being passed back. I lit one, passed a few more, and then from both sides a hand full of unlit candles were passed to me at the same time. There was nowhere left to pass them. So, I held the unlit candles in both hands, still managing to hold the lit candle between them. It entered my mind that I had come to pray that this little Armenian church would take part in lighting the hearts of the city around them with their love. Were the candles a symbolic message of assurance?

As it turned out, this little church was only steps from where I was staying, just around the corner. It was very easy to go there and pray each day. On Easter Sunday, I rose early, not wanting to miss anything. At first there were just a few people seated. At the front, about a dozen men and women in robes sang prayers and praises for hours. Little by little, people came, until again, there was standing room only, and the courtyard was filled. The priest gave a message, but everything was in Turkish, of course. How I wanted to know what he said. Afterward I kept asking about the message, until I found a couple of people who could speak to me in English. From what I could understand it came down to this—be happy, be friendly, because Christ has risen! Those were words to live by!

Each morning I went to pray. The caretaker had a friendly smile and I could hear the happy children at school. Sometimes people came in to light candles for loved ones. The light was welcoming as it flowed through the simple stained-glass windows and I felt at peace. Afterward, I would often walk along the sea or have a latte at a little café. I visited parks full of tulips, more beautiful than any gardens I had ever seen. Tulips, hyacinth, and crocus flowed down the hillsides in wonderful patterns of color and harmony, under tall trees overlooking the sea. Fountains sparkled with light, and young brides and grooms posed for pictures in the magical gardens.

In midweek I ended up at a dinner where I knew no one. It was set up at the last minute by an acquaintance who could not attend but thought I would enjoy it. The gathering only happened once a month—a good-sized group of young people from everywhere, full of life, all relatively new to the city. They had come to share God's love. I had been praying for God's great love to bless Turkey for five years; this gave me hope! I wondered if God was intentionally encouraging me during such a difficult time in my life—showing me my prayers really do matter.

In the evenings I would sit and talk with the couple who hosted me, enjoying delicious food and hospitality. At the end of the week, late Saturday night, Aza announced we were going out.

"What time is it, Aza?" I asked skeptically.

"It's 23:30, but we must go," she replied.

"I don't know; I'm pretty tired. I'm almost sixty, you know. You're young, Aza." Eleven thirty at night was late for me, and I was trying to get out of it. "But if you want to …."

"We must go! I am Muslim, but in the city where I grew up, we all know that at midnight the fire from Jerusalem will come. Don't you know this? You go to the church every day!"

She had grown up in a place where there were many Orthodox churches. She gave me a quick education online about what was about to happen, and I explained that I believed the light is inside us, if we believe.

"Yes, yes," she said. "The light is in us, and I can see it spilling out of you. Let's hurry!" and with that, this young Muslim woman took me to the Orthodox Saint Stephen's church, a block away, to a midnight candlelight service!

The next day was Easter for the Greek Orthodox church, as they follow a different calendar. It was also my last day before returning home. I went back to "my" Saint Stephens, the Armenian church, since it was my last chance. The older women, many wearing scarves on their heads, had taken me in—patting my hand and kindly motioning this way or that, when I was at a loss for what to do. After the service, again, I so wanted to know what the message was about. The women found someone who could understand my question, who then found someone else who knew enough English to answer it.

The message: We need to pursue God. He is always active in our lives with his goodness, but there is also the devil who is active and wants to deceive us. I knew God had sent me to a thriving church by the Spirit in the friendly people and the simple truth of the message. I had prayed all week for the Armenian church, throughout Turkey, to reach out with love and tell others the stories of how Jesus touches their lives. I prayed for their protection, as they are steadfast people who have suffered much. I prayed for the people of Istanbul and for the country. I prayed that God would pour out his Spirit to the precious Turkish people, who are so warm and hospitable, who have taken in so many refugees, and who need God's provision so much. I think God was telling me—"Your prayers matter."

The Sunday after I returned home from my amazing trip, the message was from the book of Acts. The death of Stephen had been the catalyst for the growth of the church. Then I remembered that the Sunday before my trip the message was also about Stephen in Acts 7—the stoning of Stephen, after he so eloquently told the story of their history and proclaimed Jesus as the Righteous One. It seemed unlikely that these messages would book-end my trip to Saint Stephen's! You see, my first husband, who had died so young, was also named Stephen. The surprise candlelight services had also marked the beginning and end of the week. On my first trip to Turkey, the woman with the basket of grapes had shown me how to light a candle in memory of my Stephen. This had been the place I prayed each day. Stephen's life and death had affected me at the deepest level—the catalyst for my passion to see others find eternal life. So many unlikely things had lined up to happen on this trip to Turkey. God touched my heart in a very personal way, when I needed it the most. For me, there is no denying God is real, cares deeply, and is active in our lives! Though evil sought to destroy, God carried me and showed me his love in an extraordinary way.

Our Role in Fighting Evil

We can all have a part in this real-life melodrama between good and evil when we demonstrate our love for God and other people. When we take seriously his call to pray and show our love to others, we *will* make a difference. When we decide to get off the sidelines and take an active role, it gets the attention of the supernatural realm, and evil may put up a stronger fight. As we actively reach out to others, there will be opposition, but we should not fear or let it derail us. Remember, we are not alone in the battle. We need help, and we have it in God, his people, and even his angels. When Joshua was to succeed Moses, God encouraged him, many times, to be strong and courageous, because he was with him. The angels have watch over us, and we can say as Elisha, "Don't be afraid. Those who are with us are more than those who are with them" (2 Kings 6:16). Jesus tells us not to be afraid and has repeatedly demonstrated his authority over evil. He teaches us to call upon his authority. Understanding this will help us continue in confidence, because we are assured God has won the battle in the long run. If we are living to reflect God's love, we are on the winning side!

When we set out to make a difference in our world, showing God's love and protection to others, we cannot fully prepare before going forward, and we cannot continue forward without further preparation. In other words, we must take a step of faith to join God in his work. We learn and are enabled, step by step, as we interact with God and each other. That preparation and process is described in the book of Ephesians by the analogy of putting on armor, a picture taken from warfare.

> Therefore put on the full armor of God, so that when the day of evil comes, you may be able to stand your ground, and after you have done everything, to stand. Stand firm then, with the belt of truth buckled around your waist, with the breastplate of righteousness in place, and with your feet fitted with the readiness that comes from the gospel of peace. In addition to all this, take up the shield of faith, with which you can extinguish all the flaming arrows of the evil one. Take the helmet of salvation and the sword of the Spirit, which is the word of God.
>
> And pray in the Spirit on all occasions with all kinds of prayers and requests. With this in mind be alert and always keep on praying for all the Lord's people. (Ephesians 6:13–18, emphasis mine)

Let's look at each metaphor; practical instruction, and protection that has proven effective in fighting evil. Each one teaches us more about taking hold of God's provisions, in his unfolding plan for our world.

The Belt of Truth

In chapter 6 we explored the importance of the Spirit of truth. Beware of how easily we can be led astray from reality or truth. Subtle lies affect our relationships and choices. Humankind is susceptible to thoughts and beliefs that are not true. Evil influences, and even our own hearts, can easily deceive us, so truth is central to upholding us, just as a belt is located to gird the center of a body. We need the Holy Spirit of truth to help us discern reality because deception is common.

We must filter everything through the main precepts in the Bible—to love and rely on God and to love and care for each other. "Show me your ways, Lord, teach me your paths. Guide me in your truth and teach me, for you are God my Savior, and my hope is in you all day long" (Psalm 25:4–5). Jesus said that the reason he was born and came in to this world was to testify to truth (John 18:37). Over and over again he says, throughout the book of John, "I tell you the truth." (Over sixty times it's recorded in the Gospel accounts.) Jesus says, "I tell you the truth," and then challenges our thinking in order to set us free. God created this complex world, and he is the ultimate source of truth.

We can start to be fortified by truth as we deal with negative and unloving areas in our own lives. God's Spirit and word awaken us to our own destructive attitudes and actions. We learn to value people and ourselves as God reveals his truth. Talk to God about your struggles, and ask him to give you wisdom. Let him know when you are sorry for bad attitudes or choices, and ask for his help to make a change. Accept the grace and forgiveness Jesus offers us. If you have never accepted the sacrifice Jesus made by going to the cross to pay for your sin, go ahead and claim it for yourself. It is at this point that you will have the Spirit of truth available as your advocate for truth!

The Breastplate of Righteousness

Righteousness protects our hearts from a fatal blow, just as a breastplate of armor would. Doing wrong is sin, and sin that is not covered brings death. When we receive the forgiveness Jesus offers us, acknowledging his payment for our sin, God then sees us as righteous. God says that he no longer remembers our sins or holds them against us (1 John 1:9; Hebrews 8:12). This is true protection from death and evil—Jesus' righteousness applied to us! Just as a breastplate protects the heart from a fatal wound, Jesus' righteousness protects us from evil and spiritual death. This is the first and most important aspect of the "breastplate of righteousness," because without it we do not have access to the second, which is becoming righteous. The Comforter and Counselor, namely the Holy Spirit of truth, whom Jesus told us would come, can now partner with us in life.

Doing wrong or having wrong done to us can break our hearts; righteousness protects our hearts. The Holy Spirit of truth comforts, heals, and teaches us to live righteously. He will teach us to be strong yet gentle, to have innocence and yet be wise. He will help us find the truth so that we better understand what Jesus would do in the situations of our lives. He enables true love. Each time we have made a decision contrary to what God teaches, deep down we feel the effects in our hearts. Righteousness, doing things God's way, protects our hearts. Likewise, when we have been hurt, repaying evil with good, rather than retaliation, guards our heart. The Spirit of truth helps us follow God and also helps us heal when we don't.

The Bible gives us a picture lesson to help us learn about righteousness of the heart. In the book of Exodus (Exodus 20 and 32–34), after Moses delivered his people from slavery, he received the Ten Commandments on Mount Sinai to guide his people. God himself met with Moses for forty days in a cloud upon the mountain, giving him instructions for his people to live righteously. "When the Lord finished speaking to Moses on Mount Sinai, he gave him the two tablets of the Testimony, the tablets of stone inscribed by the finger of God" (Exodus 31:18 NIV1984). As Moses came down the mountain, he could see that the people had already turned from their God, who had just delivered them from slavery! They were worshiping a golden calf—already breaking the first commandment that God had just given Moses. In his anger Moses threw down the tablets, breaking them. The broken tablets are a picture lesson that the law would be broken and thus bring death before our Holy God. About three thousand people were killed in the judgment that followed.

God called Moses, who was fervently praying for God's mercy, to go back up the mountain. Moses was on Mount Sinai for another forty days and nights, and once again God gave to him the Ten Commandments. The two new tablets of the Law, chiseled out by Moses and inscribed by God, were then carried down and stored in the Ark of the Covenant. God was determined to show compassion and love, making a covenant with the people. If they would trust and obey, by following his law to love God and each other, he would bless them (Deuteronomy 10–11). However, even when they knew what God expected, they still failed in their efforts to meet their part of the covenant promise.

Before Moses died at age 120, God renewed his covenant with the people, including new generations (Deuteronomy 28–30). The Old Testament goes on to record that God sent many prophets to warn and teach his people. Over and over again, the people tried to follow God's law but always failed. In the same way, as we strive to follow God's law—to love God and each other and make the right choices—in our own strength, we fail. In our failure we begin to recognize that we need help. God has a plan to keep both sides of the covenant promise.

The picture story continues in the New Testament book of Acts, but first let's set the stage as God takes action to keep our part of the covenant. Jesus, born of the Virgin Mary, lived on earth until age thirty-three, teaching the true meaning of God's law and performing many miracles of compassion, including raising people from the dead. To fulfill his destiny, he was falsely accused and willingly put to death by crucifixion to pay for our sins. Jesus' purpose was to make it possible for men and women to be declared righteous before God and receive the help of the Holy Spirit of truth. (At that point in time, humankind did not comprehend God's redemptive plan that was unfolding.)

Death could not hold Jesus in the tomb, as he is the Creator (John 1:3). On the third day, though the tomb was sealed and guarded, the giant stone had rolled away from the entrance. The women went looking for the dead body of Jesus, and an angel told them he had risen (Matthew 28:5–6; Mark 16:1–6). Jesus was and he is alive! Scripture tells us he met with and comforted his followers, and over 500 people were eyewitnesses to his resurrection (Acts 1:3; 1 Corinthians 15:1–8). Jesus told them about the kingdom of God and instructed them to expect the Spirit of truth (which they also did not yet understand). Forty days after the resurrection his followers watched as Jesus ascended to heaven (Acts 1:9–11). Just before rising into the clouds, he gave them this call and assurance:

> All authority in heaven and on earth has been given to me. Therefore go and make disciples of all nations, baptizing them in the name of the Father and of the Son and of the Holy Spirit, and teaching them to obey everything I have commanded you. And surely I am with you always, to the very end of the age. (Matthew 28:18–20)

Our picture story continues in Acts 2. On the holy day of Pentecost, which was celebrated to commemorate Moses receiving the Ten Commandments, the promised Holy Spirit of truth arrived. People from every nation were gathered in Jerusalem. The crowd heard a great wind and saw fire landing upon each person and yet not harming them! Jesus's followers began to speak languages they did not know, and the people gathered could hear what was being said in their own language. Peter spoke, quoting from the prophet Joel; "'In the last days', God says, 'I will pour out my Spirit on all people'" (Acts 2:17). About three thousand people realized and believed that Jesus was the promised Savior and received eternal life! Three thousand souls received life, the same number of people who died when the Law was given (Exodus 32:28; Acts 2:41)! From this day forward in history, the Spirit of truth, God himself, is available to dwell with us, teaching us to love and giving us firsthand help in the battle against sin and evil. The law itself could not make us righteous, but God, dwelling within human hearts, can! The law could not accomplish love from the heart, but the Spirit of God can.

> So now there isn't any condemnation for those who are in Christ Jesus. The law of the Spirit of life in Christ Jesus has set you free from the law of sin and death. God has done what was impossible for the Law, since it was weak because of selfishness. God condemned sin in the body by sending his own Son to deal with sin in the same body as humans, who are controlled by sin. He did this so that the righteous requirement of the Law might be fulfilled in us. Now the way we live is based on the Spirit, not based on selfishness. (Romans 8:1–4 CEB)

> You are our letter, written on our hearts, known and read by everyone. You show that you are Christ's letter, delivered by us. You weren't written with ink but with the spirit of the living God. You weren't written on tablets of stone but on tablets of human hearts.
>
> This is the confidence we have through Christ in the presence of God. It isn't that we ourselves are qualified to claim that anything came from us. No, our qualification came from God. He has qualified us as ministers of a new covenant, not based on what is written but on the Spirit,

because what is written kills, but the Spirit gives life.
(2 Corinthians 3:2–6 CEB)

Thus, our righteousness is twofold, because now, through Jesus, we can be declared righteous by God, and we also have help to become righteous through the Holy Spirit's presence in our lives. We have the help we need to do the right thing, to make good choices, and to obtain the comfort our hearts need, if we choose to embrace it. The Spirit helps us not to judge, as we apply to others the grace and love of God that we ourselves have received. Once God reveals truth to us, we will have to make adjustments. To go forward in confidence, we will need to change, aligning ourselves to what God teaches us through his word. Our righteousness is found only in Christ, who frees us from sin and guilt. Righteousness is not found in following a list of rules and regulations, but rather in the freedom of aligning our hearts with the heart of God, by the help of the Spirit of truth.

Feet Fitted with the Readiness that Comes from the Gospel of Peace

God tells us that our life on earth can be like running a race for him (Hebrews 12:1). To run the race, we need to be fitted with the right shoes— the gospel of peace. Jesus's sacrificial death and victorious resurrection on our behalf enable sinful men and women to find peace with God—this is the gospel of peace! We need to "put on" this gospel, to be ready to work with God. Then others will see the truth and light living in us, as we run the race we have been given.

Jesus explained that he did not come so we would have peace on earth at the present time, as many of his followers thought. Rather, he came that we could have peace with God through his death and resurrection. We need to be at peace with our Creator in order to have peace with others. Trusting Jesus, putting on the gospel of peace, prepares us to run the race. We are no longer fighting or hiding from God in our rebellious and insecure state, but we choose to work or run alongside him until his work on earth is accomplished. We are on God's team! He helps us in our race, giving us strength and endurance along the way. Just as in a relay, we run our part of the race, passing on and proclaiming the good news of Jesus's redemption and peace to the people along our path of life. They in turn, go forward, passing true love to future generations.

The Shield of Faith

> "Now faith is confidence in what we hope for and assurance about what we do not see. (Hebrews 11:1)

Do you believe God exists and created the universe? Do you believe in his promises? Do you want to believe? Our faith in God (and what he teaches us in his word and by experience) is what brings us to the point of believing the gospel of peace, the good news of Jesus. Faith means we believe God. At first it may just be a desire to believe God is there for us—perhaps seeing a sunset and sensing something more—a peace, a wonder that there may be a creator. We call out to him when we are in trouble or need. It might be a search for purpose. We begin to seek him. Though we cannot see God, we believe that he exists from the evidence of creation and the love of his people, and through our experiences we start learning to trust him. As our faith takes action, responding to his love and direction, we experience God. Tiny seeds of faith grow into powerful family faith. This is how the "love tree" grows.

> Without faith it is impossible to please God, because anyone who comes to him must believe that he exists and that he rewards those who earnestly seek him. (Hebrews 11:6)

Faith is believing God wants the best for us and can be trusted. It is acknowledging his power, trusting his love, and acting on his word. It is believing that he loves us and was willing to come from heaven to lay down his life to rescue us. Faith in Jesus is our shield from death and from all that the evil one sends our way. Faith calls on the power and protection of God and grows as we experience his provision. God allows difficulties in our lives, knowing we will learn from them—to trust, to love, and to grow in wisdom. Faith helps us persevere in life through the hard times, and it grows as we experience God's activity and care for us on a personal level.

God also gives faith as a gift to help others, as we pray and act on their behalf. Faith, demonstrated by our prayers for others, can soften hearts, help shield them from evil, and help them heal. When we live in active faith, we find protection and courage to fight the good fight, living for God and caring for those around us.

The Helmet of Salvation

A helmet protects us from a potentially fatal blow to the head. Salvation gives protection to both your life and mind. Faith in the gospel of peace brings you salvation, saving you from eternal death which is eternal separation from God. Since God is the source of truth, love, and light, eternal separation would mean eternal deception and darkness; a place without the true warmth of love. The Bible teaches that the blood of Jesus—the Son of God and the Son of Man, the perfect and sinless Lamb—is applied to our lives when we turn to him for salvation. It covers us, just as the blood of a lamb without defect was applied to the door frame of the Hebrew people at Passover, so that death would pass over (Exodus 12). Jesus's blood was poured out for all people, from every race and nation under heaven.

The Bible makes it clear that God wants all people to turn to him and be saved from eternal death. "The Lord is not slow in keeping his promise, as some understand slowness. Instead he is patient with you, not wanting anyone to perish, but everyone to come to repentance" (2 Peter 3:9).

The helmet of salvation also protects our minds. The Spirit of truth now can help us guard our thoughts from the influence of evil. He protects us by helping us focus on what is good, true, and beneficial. The Spirit brings to our minds God's loving principles and his words.

The Holy Spirit is calling out to you to accept the free gift of salvation. Don't allow evil to strike a fatal blow to your life; put on the helmet of salvation. Without it, we do not have the protection and power necessary to successfully fight evil within our minds and within our lives. We need the protection of salvation to fight on behalf of the lives of others as well.

The Sword of the Spirit, which Is the Word of God

God speaks to us through his word, the Bible, giving us practical instructions to improve our relationships and guiding us in our quest to live fulfilled. The Bible teaches us much about who God is and what he wants for us. The Spirit can use the Word of God to show us areas where we do not trust God or where *our* idea of love does not match up with God's. God has recorded story after story, common to us all, to teach us. We begin to understand the universal and historical vulnerability of mankind to doubt God's love and be led astray. The Bible can be overwhelming at first, yet from beginning to end, it's the story of God's enduring love for the people he created. It tells of God's unfailing sacrificial love and his plan to redeem mankind. The Word of God is often the source the Spirit of truth uses to challenge, enlighten, and change us.

It is a book of history with many layers and stories within the story that only God could interweave. It was written by forty different authors from many walks of life. Each writer, reflecting an individual personality, was inspired by God and assisted by the Holy Spirit to write truth. In this way God gave his message to the world. Over and over again, people who earnestly study the Bible increase their faith in God, because it would be impossible for this book to be so amazingly cohesive without God's supernatural direction. Sixty-six books woven together with picture after picture of God's redeeming plan for the world. A plan that unfolds with the miracle of God in us. There are hundreds of prophecies written in the Bible that are fulfilled by future events—events now recorded in history! This is one evidence of the reality of God and the authority of his written word.

Beyond God's assurance through the evidence of fulfilled prophecy, the living Word of God has amazing power to change lives. Read it story by story, chapter by chapter, and verse by verse. As we spend time thinking about what God is saying to us, and then adjust our lives to it, we prepare ourselves for our futures. Marvel at the way God reveals the truth to you in the days ahead. Memorize your favorite verses; it is amazing how they will pop into your mind just when you need them. God's word, like a sword, will fight off evil that is seeking to influence your mind, your heart, and ultimately your life. Try starting with the books of Genesis and John, if you are new to reading the Bible. Ask God to help you discover *his* plan for your life.

> All scripture is God-breathed and is useful for teaching,
> rebuking, correcting and training in righteousness, so that

the servant of God may be thoroughly equipped for every good work. (2 Timothy 3:16–17)

The word of God is alive and active. Sharper than any double-edged sword, it penetrates even to dividing soul and spirit, joints and marrow; it judges the thoughts and attitudes of the heart. (Hebrews 4:12)

The Spirit of truth helps us to understand the comprehensive principles taught in the Bible and to live them out. We need instruction from the word of God to learn truth, to live right, to grow in faith, and to fight evil.

Prayer and Fighting Evil

The apostle Paul, in the book of Ephesians, explains the need for believers to wear spiritual armor. Then he adds the following instruction:

And pray in the Spirit on all occasions with all kinds of prayers and requests. With this in mind, be alert and always keep on praying for all the Lord's people. (Ephesians 6:18)

Prayer plays an important role in the life of God's people. Evil is constantly working to keep people in darkness, both within our thoughts and our circumstances. *Prayer welcomes the Holy Spirit's presence to the situation and helps block the access of evil in the spiritual realm.* Praying is the first step to getting involved in the action, because as we invite God into each situation, including the tasks he has called us to, we are fortified by his power and protection. God's design is partnership with humanity. Talking to God shows our desire to communicate and personally know him. It activates us to work alongside him, showing our willing trust and reliance on him. As God calls us, we need to call on God. Let him know you are willing and are looking to him for direction and protection and strength. Prayer unleashes his unmatched power.

Our prayers direct and protect others from evil as well. Prayers for people who are far from God can soften their hearts and help them understand truth. Like God's word, it is both "armor" and "weapon" for fighting the good fight. When you see others doing God's good work, fortify them by your prayers. Over the years, I have heard stories of people being moved to pray for someone, out of the blue, only later to find out that the person was in a difficult or dangerous situation just at that hour. Jesus is interceding for us (Romans 8:34), on our behalf, and the Spirit of God whispers, calling us to help and to pray! We must constantly call on and rely on God to be effective in our homes, communities, and our world.

> Let your gentleness be evident to all. The Lord is near. Do not be anxious about anything, but in every situation, by prayer and petition, with thanksgiving, present your requests to God. And the peace of God, which transcends all understanding, will guard your hearts and minds in Jesus Christ. (Philippians 4:5–7)

Think about these verses. When we become anxious or frightened or feel things are not in our control, that's when we're most likely to become angry, lose our patience, lash out, or do something we'll regret. We need to remember the truth that God is near and wants to help us; believe it! Having this assurance will motivate us to talk to him about the situation and to rely on him, allowing the Holy Spirit to pour out gentleness through us.

Jesus taught us about prayer through his example and teachings. His followers asked him how to pray, and he taught them what is known as "The Lord's Prayer," recorded in Matthew 6:5–15 and Luke 11:1–13; 18:1–14. Let's take a look in relation to fighting evil.

"'Our Father in heaven, hallowed be your name, your kingdom come, your will be done, on earth as it is in heaven'" (Matthew 6:9–10). The prayer starts with the call to fight evil! We acknowledge his name is hallowed, honored, and holy, having faith that God is completely good and all powerful. Then we ask for his loving will to be accomplished in our world (as it is in heaven). We are asking God to fight evil on earth—to conquer sin and the schemes of evil within ourselves, our community, and our world. It is our invitation to join him in that fight as he reveals truth to us. We are asking for his help with the personal sin that stops us from having a productive life and the collective sin that affects our community's well-being. Seeking his will is our focus.

"'Give us today our daily bread. And forgive us our debts, as we also forgive our debtors'" (Matthew 6:11–12). In order for his loving will to be accomplished, we need to be fed with both physical and spiritual food. He cares about our needs—food, shelter, love, and security. He is the ultimate source of provision, both physical and spiritual. God cares about all of our needs, but the spiritual aspects of our lives are his greatest concerns (Matthew 6:25–34; Luke 12:1–7). "Forgive us our debts." Forgiveness from our sin saves us, and enables us to gain the spiritual provision we need to fight evil. Confession is part of the process of personal renewal and change. "As we also forgive or debtors." Forgiving others, extending grace instead of revenge, breaks the cycle of evil. To have the power to forgive, we need God's help, and so, we ask for it.

"'And lead us not into temptation, but deliver us from the evil one'" (Matthew 6:13). God knows we are in a treacherous world, tempted and impacted by evil. He tells us to ask for his help and deliverance, to seek him. His kingdom and glory will come about when we see the eternal fruit of fighting evil. In that day, it will be like the vision in chapter one. Love is in the air and we breathe it freely. Until then we join him in the fight, experiencing victories big and small, personal and societal, along the way.

Jesus also taught us to be persistent and bold, before God in prayer, in order to fight evil. In Luke 11:5–13 and Luke 18:1–8 he taught us not to give up. Perhaps this has something to do with the intensity of the battle, which often we cannot see. God loves us, and Jesus has already determined the outcome of the final battle by his sacrifice for our sakes, yet our prayers play a role in each victory. Don't give up, keep praying, and be sure to respond to God's "still small voice" with obedience.

Praying with the right motive, and taking action when we are called, are very important. Jesus warns us that prayer should never be uttered to impress others. In Isaiah 58, Matthew 6:5–17, and Luke 18:9–14, God warns that prayer without turning our heart to God and obediently caring for the people he puts in our path is not effective. Prayer to make oneself *look* righteous is meaningless. However, the prayer of someone who earnestly seeks God and shows compassionate care for others is very powerful.

John 17 records Jesus's prayer for his followers both for the present time and also those who would follow him in the future. You can hear God's love and concern. His prayer for our protection from evil is heartfelt, as he knows he leaves the earth soon. He prays for our unity, and that we would make God and his love known to the world. Reflect on these verses. Take note of other times when Jesus prayed, as you read the Gospel accounts recorded in Matthew, Mark, Luke, and John. Jesus took time to get away to talk and listen to the Father. He prayed publicly and privately, for himself, for others, and for us. Jesus still prays for us (Romans 8:34); not only did he teach about the importance of prayer, but he set an example.

I have experienced the answers to hundreds of prayers throughout my life, and I know you can too. Most likely you already have. Yet we may not *always* see the answer within our lifetime. Sometimes God has something better, and other times it will come in the future. God teaches us to be persistent and have confidence. Wonderful surprises will be waiting for us in eternity! "Don't be afraid." Prayer is the key.

God has proven faithful through all of my life's trials and everything evil has sent my way. Though physically I am not strong, God's strength has given me courage and perseverance to fight the good fight. He has enabled me to take part in the battle against evil that is still raging in our world. We all have a part to play and the opportunity to take hold of the protection that God provides for us and apply it to our lives. We can all care for and pray for the lives of others. Prepare yourself by putting on the armor of protection: truth, righteousness, the gospel of peace, faith, salvation, learning the word of God, and applying it with prayer. God is love; he is pure and just and reaches out to imperfect humans with longsuffering and grace. He desires for us to accept his grace and love and extend it to others, becoming heroes in the battle between good and evil. Ask, and look to the Spirit of truth to direct you each day. Discover your purpose—doing your part to defeat evil. God is with you. We all have a part in the battle, but God's already won the war!

> When Jesus received the drink, Jesus said, *"It is finished."*
> With that he bowed his head and gave up his spirit.
> (John 19:30, italics added)

> At that moment the curtain of the temple was torn in two
> from top to bottom. The earth shook and the rocks split.
> (Matthew 27:51)

And when the centurion, who stood there in front of Jesus, heard his cry and saw how he died, he said, "Surely this man was the son of God!" (Mark 15:39)

Why are you looking for the living among the dead? He is not here: he has risen! Remember how he told you when he was still with you in Galilee: "The Son of Man must be delivered into the hands of sinful men, be crucified and on the third day be raised again." (Luke 24:5–7)

Jesus came and stood among them and said, "Peace be with you!" After he said this, he showed him his hands and side. The disciples were overjoyed when they saw the Lord. Again Jesus said, "Peace be with you! As the Father has sent me, I am sending you." (John 20:19–21)

When he saw the crowds, he had compassion on them, because they were harassed and helpless, like sheep without a shepherd. Then he said to his disciples, "The harvest is plentiful but the workers are few. Ask the Lord of the harvest, therefore, to send out workers into his harvest field." (Matthew 9:36–38)

> Even though I walk
>   through the darkest valley,
> I will fear no evil,
>   for you are with me;
> your rod and your staff,
>   they comfort me. (Psalm 23:4)

Be strong and courageous. Do not be afraid or terrified because of them, for the Lord your God goes with you; he will never leave you nor forsake you. (Deuteronomy 31:6)

The Lord is faithful, and he will strengthen you and protect you from the evil one. (2 Thessalonians 3:3)

Discussion:

1. What are some examples of the battle between good and evil in our world?
2. Who does the Bible tell us is our true enemy (see Ephesians 6:12)? Give a reason why this might be important to remember.
3. Describe each part of the armor God made available to us and how it helps in fighting evil.
   a. Belt of truth
   b. Breastplate of righteousness
   c. Feet fitted with the gospel of peace
   d. Shield of faith
   e. Helmet of salvation
   f. Sword of the Spirit which is the word of God
4. Read Luke 11:1–13 and 18:1–14 as a group. What did Jesus teach us about prayer?
5. Read Isaiah 58:1–11. What are some possible reasons that God may not answer our prayers?
6. Describe a time when you felt caught up in the battle between good and evil.

CHAPTER 10

Perseverance

Passion broke through,
Sweet purpose grew.
But so weary by autumn,
"What good can we do?"

Know that God has you,
Take time to rest.
But don't give up the battle,
Whether warfare or test.

With faith, we go forward,
Our hope to prevail.
God's promise to us—
His love never fails!

Let us not become weary in doing good, for at the proper
time we will reap a harvest if we do not give up.
—Galatians 6:9

"Goodbye, old farm. You were good to me. I hope I've been good to you."

Dad had tears in his eyes as he stood at the car door, the last time he would see his beloved farm. He had saved the old farm, and I told him so. The stone house, built in 1735, needed much work to restore. The fields would have been long overgrown. Dad was not a big man in stature but was a lanky hard worker. He was not perfect but was a kind man of perseverance. The day Mom and Dad closed on the house, they sat on the dilapidated front porch and looked at each other.

"What have we gotten ourselves into?" they said to each other.

Then Dad got up, "I don't know, but we better get to work!"

He told me that story many times in his last days, when dementia kept recent moments a blur but brought back deep-rooted memories. He had poured his life into that farm and house restoration. Just to keep the ancient International Harvester tractor going took more determination and ingenuity than I would ever have; even rigging pulleys from beams to lift it. Working a dairy farm with little help while commuting to a full-time job shows determination. Dad may have been naive about what lay ahead when he started, but he did well, and it was perseverance that made an extraordinary life for us all.

Our life is rarely—perhaps never—as easy as we think it will be. In life we need grit! We need God's help to be steadfast—getting up each day, doing the work we are given, overcoming hardship, obstacles, and disappointments to achieve our goals. Our relationships—with friends, coworkers, marriage partners, or our children—take commitment, to respect and support each other, despite each other's shortcomings. Believing a promise of God, despite circumstances to the contrary, takes perseverance in faith. We set our mind and develop our heart to persevere, as we rely on God's love, guidance, and help.

Perseverance is needed in everyday life. Even more so as we decide to get off the sidelines and fight against evil on behalf of others. At first, experiencing God's hand as he guides us to enrich lives or accomplish a goal is exciting. Inevitably, what is energizing at first becomes exhausting and even overwhelming. First, most things that are worthwhile take a lot of effort. Second, there is a spiritual battle going on that we cannot see, although we can see the effects and often feel them. It is important to rely on God and not give up! When God gives you a task, mission, or calling, and you have moved forward in faith, do not let doubt and weariness stop you from fighting the good fight, until God has completed his work through you.

People often make the mistake of thinking that if God gives us a task or mission, he will pave the way so that everything goes smoothly, but that is not biblical. Read chapter 11 in Hebrews about all the great men and women in Old Testament history who took action in faith. At the end of the chapter we read, "These were all commended for their faith, yet none of them received what had been promised" (verse 39). Wow, it did not work out for any of them as they expected! God did fulfill his promises to them, but not until after their life on earth had ended. For example, we know that Abraham did become the father of many nations, even though he did not have his first child until he was eighty-six years old and his second at age one hundred (Genesis 16:16; 17:18–20; 21:5; 22:17–18; Romans 4:16–17). Moses himself never entered the Promised Land (Deuteronomy 32:52), though he spent forty years of his life leading the people to it.

Hebrews goes on to say, "God had planned something better for us so that only together with us would they be made perfect" (Hebrews 11:40). Would we say that Abraham and Moses were not successful in God's eyes? Of course not! God was pleased, even though they each had moments they would not be proud of. They needed the redemption Christ accomplished applied to their lives, just as we do. But as we look at their life stories in the Old Testament, we can see a process of going forward in faith, time and time again. These men and women of faith kept believing, no matter the circumstances, and kept acting on that belief. They talked to God when they had doubts, expecting and waiting for his response, instead of turning from him. We also need to go forward in faith, talk to God, learn from our mistakes, and go forward again. We can look to God for direction and trust God for the outcome. There is a battle that's real—a battle that is opposing efforts to bring love and life to those who need it. God's call is often not easy, so depend on him and do your best. Looking for the good and giving thanks in the face of life's difficulties has power. Look for God's activity, focus in, and ask him to empower your efforts. Faith and perseverance bring great blessings!

Persevering throughout the hardships and challenges of life changes our character; we become more like Jesus. This is the process of sanctification—becoming, step by step, people of good character whom God can use—people who listen to the Spirit of truth and put God's purposes first. We are transformed day by day, filled with God's grace and love. For all of us, no matter where our lives fall in history, we are not yet the holy people God promises we will be in the future.

You could put it like this: We all need some pruning to have good fruit. Jesus said, "I am the true vine, and my Father is the gardener. He cuts off every branch in me that bears no fruit, while every branch that does bear fruit he prunes so that it will be even more fruitful." He goes on to say, "I am the vine; you are the branches. If you remain in me and I in you, you will bear much fruit; apart from me you can do nothing" (John 15:1–2, 5; see vs. 1–12).

Everything of lasting value is done in connection with God! He is the powerful sustainer of life and the compassionate source of true love. Allowing God to make changes in our lives, to prune us and remove the dead branches, enables us to grow in character and become fruitful in loving others. Jesus is interceding on our behalf in the spiritual realm. The person of the Holy Spirit is available to guide us, step by step. God's activity in our lives is necessary to make a lasting impact on our world. Things are not always going to go smoothly, which should be no surprise. Trials in which we persevere by faith are often where God does some deep pruning. Reaching out and loving others well are not exempt, but rather some of the richest soil where some of the most fruitful pruning can be done. Some people give up, becoming bitter or disillusioned, but others turn to God, persevere, and become the most mature, beautiful, and loving people.

Commitment is the first step toward perseverance. If God is prompting you to make a change in your life, commit to pray for God's help each day. If you have made a commitment in a relationship, ask God's help to make the most of it. If you sense God's direction in your life, commit to follow it. Jesus warns us, "The harvest is plentiful but the workers are few" (Matthew 9:37). Everywhere, from your home to a distant land, there is opportunity to demonstrate love. God tells us to pray for workers. Pray that hearts would be moved to action. Find the place God wants *you* to work.

Once I heard a missionary to Africa say he was weary of other people's good ideas. On a trip home to the United States he was addressing the lack of commitment he saw in the church. If you have an idea, God is usually calling you to get involved in the effort. Investigate to see how God is working in that area. Is he inviting you to join him in his work? You need to commit! Whether a task to support others, or a life mission, you need perseverance to see it through. Even something as simple as forging a relationship by meeting with a coworker for lunch once a week takes commitment, or else other things get in the way. Nothing is more important to you and your family than being in the center of God's will. Perseverance and commitment help to keep us there.

There is an unexpected secret to perseverance—rest. God tells us to take time to rest and to rest in him. If we don't take some time to enjoy our lives, we burn out. Take a day each week to rest. Enjoying the comfort of a warm breeze, the sounds of nature, time alone with God, time with family and friends—these moments calm our minds and fortify our souls. Thankfulness is renewed and refills our hearts with strength.

There is another dimension to our rest. Jesus said, "Come to me, all you who are weary and burdened, and I will give you rest. Take my yoke upon you and learn from me, for I am gentle and humble in heart, and you will find rest for your souls. For my yoke is easy and my burden is light" (Matthew 11:28–30). The imagery of a yoke is one of being guided. There is still a burden, work to plow or plant, but it will not be too heavy because we are relying on God to guide and provide for us daily. The burden becomes lighter as our souls find rest in God. After saying this, Jesus went on to pick some grain to eat, challenging what the Pharisees were teaching about the Sabbath—that activity of any kind, even healing, on the Sabbath day was unlawful. He wanted to get at the heart of the matter. Jesus taught that the Sabbath day was made for the good of man, not man for the Sabbath (Mark 2:27). The Sabbath, in part, symbolizes loving acceptance of our dependency on God and wholehearted trust in his care for us as our provider. Furthermore, without resting in his guidance, we cannot accomplish his will or the work that he plans for us. *Vine's Dictionary* explains it beautifully:

> Christ's "rest" is not a "rest" from work, but in work, "not the rest of inactivity but of the harmonious workings of all the faculties and affections—of will, heart, imagination, conscience—because each has found in God the ideal sphere for its satisfaction and development" (J. Patrick in *Hastings' Bible Dictionary*).

To rest in him, as we do our God-given work, can take a lifetime to learn. In resting we persevere.

The men and women of faith, listed in Hebrews 11, inspire and assure us. Their hope was not fulfilled within their lifetime, yet each persevered in faith and obedience. None of them were perfect, but each believed God is faithful. The lives of our most prominent historical figures, such as Abraham Lincoln and Martin Luther King Jr., have similar characteristics. They each had an unshakable belief in a God-given idea or principle and perseverance within their own lives that was above and beyond. Their lives were not easy; they were not perfect; but they trusted in God's direction and persevered. These are the lives that make great strides for humankind. Another such man was William Carey. His amazing story is another true-life example. God has a plan; don't give up!

William Carey, a poor English shoemaker, believed with all his heart that all the world should have the Bible in their language. He passionately believed those living in Asia should have the opportunity to know Jesus loved them personally and set his life course to that end, though the task seemed impossible, and he met constant resistance. Carey trained to become a pastor, inspired others, set sail twice (the first time he was delayed), and worked for forty years in India. He buried a five-year-old son and two wives. His second wife was a blessing in his work, but the first was overwhelmed by the life they'd chosen.

Throughout all his trials he remained patient and gentle with people. Even after working long days in a factory in order to provide for his family, he worked tirelessly to translate the Bible, set up schools, and teach. Eventually, he translated the whole Bible in three different dialects and also contributed to other translations—work that in itself takes amazing perseverance. In a warehouse fire in 1812 his manuscripts were destroyed, which he took very hard, but he determinedly translated them again! He made an impact on India, not only by translating God's word, but also fighting against such practices as widow burning. He called people to be responsible for the fate of others and took up the call himself.

Though he may have felt like a failure in his early years, his life sparked a movement in history, which in turn has enabled today's Asian nationals to take up the cause that he and many others lived and died for. Their perseverance is even now taking root in the lives of others, ordinary people who lived extraordinary lives. (Story is adapted from Ruth Ann Tucker's book, *From Jerusalem to Irian Jaya*.) William Cary persevered in work and life, even after great loss. Perhaps his work was part of what helped him go on after so much tragedy. He believed God had called him to bring God's word of life to the people of India.

William Carey faced deep heartache and vast disappointment. It took a lifetime to accomplish his God-given goals. Men and women such as these give me inspiration as I face hardship. Though God has allowed grief and difficulty to come my way, he has also helped me persevere through tragedy, sickness, and hard times. He has given my spirit comfort, provided me with blessings, and he cares about my deepest needs. Resting in my God-given work has brought me peace. There are silver linings in the storms of my life.

Over the years, my tears grew fewer, as if they were bottled. (I'm not sure that's a good thing; probably not.) Yet I breathe, look to the light, and go forward. I've imagined Jesus wiping away my teardrops when I finally come home to him. No one comforts me like my Father God. As I've experienced the Spirit's comfort, I've learned to trust God even more, seeing his care over and over again. In that trust, though it is hard to understand *why* tragedy strikes or hard times persist, we discover more of God's transforming, healing power and love. God helps us handle the sorrows of our lives and heals our pain. He teaches us with patience and love. And he promises something more, "beauty from the ashes," gifts in our own lives and in the lives of others, for everyone who wants to be his child. I have observed over time that the people who have gone through the most are often the people who make the biggest impact in the lives of others. True love is not easy to learn, but its results are beautiful!

Therefore, since we are surrounded by such a great cloud of witnesses, let us throw off everything that hinders and the sin that so easily entangles. And let us run with perseverance the race marked out for us, fixing our eyes on Jesus, the pioneer and perfecter of our faith. For the joy set before him he endured the cross, scorning its shame, and sat down at the right hand of the throne of God. Consider him who endured such opposition from sinners, so that you will not grow weary and lose heart. (Hebrews 12:1–3)

For everything that was written in the past was written to teach us, so that through the endurance taught in the Scriptures and the encouragement they provide we might have hope.

May the God who gives endurance and encouragement give you the same attitude of mind toward each other that Christ Jesus had, so that with one mind and one voice you may glorify the God and Father of our Lord Jesus Christ.

Accept one another, then, just as Christ accepted you, in order to bring praise to God. (Romans 15:4–7)

We continually ask God to fill you with the knowledge of his will through all the wisdom and understanding that the Spirit gives, so that you might live a life worthy of the Lord and please him in every way: bearing fruit in every good work, growing in the knowledge of God, being strengthened with all his power according to his glorious might so that you may have great endurance and patience, and giving joyful thanks to the Father, who has qualified you to share in the inheritance of his holy people in the kingdom of light. (Colossians 1:9–12)

Discussion:

1. Have you ever experienced *not* having things go the way you planned when you set out to do something good? Share your experience. How were you able to face the setback?
2. Has God ever used a trial in your life to prepare you for a future opportunity?
3. Share about a time in your life when you needed to persevere to accomplish a goal or endure a trial.
4. Has God ever pruned something from your life that helped you to later "bear fruit"?
5. Read Romans 15:1–13. Why is perseverance often related to our relationships?

   Paul is asking the Jewish believers to accept the Gentiles, not by insisting they follow Jewish culture, but by the grace and hope of the gospel.

   Who is the Root of Jesse?

   By what power are these two groups asked to accept each other?
6. Is there anyone you admire for their perseverance? Do they inspire you, and if so, how?

CHAPTER 11

Embrace Life Now

A child longs to grow up. *Then I can …*
A teen longs for independence. *Then I can …*
A university student longs to graduate. *Then I can …*
A parent longs for some rest. *Then I can …*
A worker longs to retire. *Then I can …*
The old long to be young again. *If only I could …*

There is a time for everything, and a season for every activity under the heavens.

—Ecclesiastes 3:1

Moreover, no one knows when their hour will come.

—Ecclesiastes 9:12

Stephen was still young—only twenty-nine—when he died unexpectedly. Let me share what was most exceptional about him: Stephen loved his life! He was one of seven children and enjoyed people. He loved to gather with friends—in our homes, out to hear a local band, or a group camping trip. Yet he also treasured quiet time in nature to recharge. He loved time tending his garden. He noticed the little things—a new bud on the almond tree, the calm of a warm summer day, a snowflake on the window, or the taste of his coffee. How he treasured the smiles of his children! He loved each day, each moment, and made the most of them. He truly embraced now. I am so glad he did.

I want to be like him, enjoying each day. As I look back, I was always anxious for the next thing—for school to start, for summer break, wishing I was in high school. But then I skipped a year to get off to college. I could not wait to be independent and start a career. But then I wished for more free time and fewer financial worries. Even now, I still struggle to settle in and be content with each day. And yet when I live in the moment, that's when I experience peace and joy.

We can either wish our life away or live in the moment, enjoying the people and beauty around us. From birth to death we go through different stages and circumstances, each with its own set of joys, responsibilities, and unique opportunities. Accepting and even embracing each phase of life is a wonderful way to live. Some phases of life are hard. Yet rarely is there not a touch of beauty in the midst of the work or the pain. Knowing that no situation of our life is a surprise to God and that he is always working for our good helps us trust God and go forward. No matter our situation or what evil sends our way, God is with us.

Embrace each season from childhood to old age. Learn and grow, follow and lead, work and rest. Each season has its advantages and enjoyable moments, and each has its difficulties. Each teaches us something more about love. There are new people who will add to our lives and whose lives will be impacted by us. Throughout each season of life, value relationships, making people a priority. Commit to make a difference in the lives of those around you. Be mindful to take the time to help and encourage. Make special plans that will recharge your spirit and bring happiness to others. Enjoy celebrations and mark milestones with family and friends. Reach for your God-given dreams, one day at a time. *You* have value and significance in every phase of life.

Solomon, a great king, the son of King David, was blessed with both wisdom and riches, yet he asks in the beautiful book of Ecclesiastes, "What does it all mean? Will my fortune or wisdom help me in the end? Am I any happier than those who work for me? What accomplishments are important?" A king, world-renowned for his wisdom, made his observation: "I know there is nothing better for people than to be happy and to do good while they live" (Ecclesiastes 3:12). King Solomon questioned the meaning of life and concluded that what makes life worth living is being thankfully content and caring for others! "Godliness with contentment is great gain" (1 Timothy 6:6).

Through each stage and position in life, it's crucial to understand who God is and the power he holds. That's why the Bible tells us, "The fear of the Lord is the beginning of wisdom; all who follow his precepts have good understanding" (Psalm 111:10). God's precepts are his overriding governing principles of love and justice. Why should we fear a loving God? Perhaps because he is creator and holds all of life in his hands. He holds my life in his hands; it makes me feel safe. But for others that is terrifying. God's love and justice will not be ignored. He is all-powerful and will punish the unrepentant who align themselves with evil. In biblical accounts, God shields us from the power of his full presence and visions are overwhelmingly met with fear (Exodus 19:16-23, 33:18–23; Isaiah 6:4–5; Matthew 17:1–7).

Thankfully, God is abundantly compassionate and absolutely good! There are over one hundred references to his goodness and compassion in the Bible. Other writings, such as the Quran (also containing over one hundred references), acclaim God's goodness and compassion as well. When we have faith that we can trust God, we begin to open up our lives to him. We learn it is safe to surrender ourselves to his plans on a personal level. It is there that we find contentment in the simple pleasures of life and satisfaction in our work. The security of God's love removes our fears, freeing us to love others. Solomon tells us there is nothing more worthwhile than this simple childlike happiness.

For all men and women, eventually their days on earth will come to an end. Whether or not we embrace God's activity in our lives affects our eternal destiny. God and his people choose each other. A true love relationship is not possible without free will. "We love because he first loved us" (1 John 4:19), and "God so loved the world that he gave his one and only Son, that whoever believes in him shall not perish but have eternal life" (John 3:16); God proclaims his love and acts on our behalf! God is involved in our lives, calling us to trust and believe. In trusting we are adopted into God's family, and our eternal destiny is secure. Near-death experience supports the claim that we will live beyond death. What is waiting in the world beyond? God's hope is for all of us to join his family tree—that we would become his children and live in a wonderful world forever more. It comes with a commitment to honor and trust God, shown by our desire to live by his principles of love and justice. If we are willing, he promises to accomplish that within us. He is patient! He gives us this life on earth to learn to trust him and find our way home.

Embracing each season helps us grasp the lessons of life more effectively. We learn that God's principles and promises are true through the circumstances of our lives and outcome of our actions. God gives glimpses of his active presence, teaching us through nature, the Spirit of truth, his word, and the Spirit-led lives of those around us. His power is beyond our comprehension, and his love is unmatched! Trusting God, *his power* and *his love*, will help us make good choices and act wisely—understanding that if we disregard God and his precepts, we have reason to fear his judgment. For some people, this fear is the first step.

It is never, ever too late! God sees the big picture, and our understanding is very limited. We will never go wrong trusting him; it is the wisest decision we can make. As we follow him, we learn to love, becoming rich in character. With a newfound wisdom and hope, we realize as King Solomon did, "A good name is better than fine perfume, and the day of death better than the day of birth" (Ecclesiastes 7:1).

God is preparing us for that day. Jesus is described with the imagery of a good shepherd, one who carries his lambs on his shoulders and goes after his lost sheep (Psalm 23; Isaiah 40:11; Matthew 18:10–14; John 10:1–16). Like us, his follower Thomas wanted to know the way home (John 14:1–5). Jesus answered, "I am the way and the truth and the life. No one comes to the Father except through me" (John 14:6). If we are willing, he will guide and sometimes even carry us home to our Father, like a shepherd who cares for his sheep. Along the journey he will lead us to places and situations where we can be fed.

Each season and situation of our lives is a time and place to prepare us—a place for us to learn the value of relying on our creator. Jesus said that doing his Father's will was his food (John 4:32–35). He knows we are "fed" by doing God's will—"feeding" others. Our faith and character grow as we display God's love and teach his truth, serving others with our lives. Like a little hummingbird, we are fed by the sweet nectar of love as we carry it to others, that they too may experience a healthy, abundant, and eternal life.

The last morning Jesus spent with his followers (on earth), he made them a fresh fish breakfast on the beach. He fed them. Then, knowing he was soon to ascend to heaven, Jesus appealed to Peter to "feed and care for his sheep." Three times Jesus asked Simon Peter, "Do you truly love me? … Feed my lambs." "Do you truly love me? … Take care of my sheep." "Do you love me? … Feed my sheep." The whole passage, found in John 21, is the last story John records.

Peter was hurt by Jesus repeatedly questioning his love. Yet it was for an important purpose: Peter would never forget what was most important to Jesus—the teaching and care of his people! Peter became the first teacher of the New Covenant of love, established by Jesus giving himself for us. Likewise, our own hurts can be used to help others when we turn to God. His love heals us, and he uses our past to impress on us the importance of reaching out and caring for others. As we experience God's presence and activity in our lives, we can share our experience and our love, leading others to Jesus. He is their "food," their sustainer, the "bread of life" (John 6:35, 47–51). There is nothing more important to God. He created each man, woman, and child and loves them all! Over and over again, he tells us if we truly love him, we need to care for others. Read Matthew 25:31–46 if you have any doubt about God's priorities (the passage is both beautiful and sobering). God's priority is people!

Don't let life pass you by, just drifting through. Be intentional about your choices and priorities in each season of your life. Decide that your life will make a difference in the battle between good and evil, which still rages on earth. Let God enable you to overcome fear and act in true love.

He is patient with us. "The Lord [God] is not slow in keeping his promise, as some understand slowness. Instead he is patient with you, not wanting anyone to perish, but everyone to come to repentance" (2 Peter 3:9). God invites us all to believe, to trust him, and to work with him. He invites us all to rest in his love. He wants us to pay attention—to be aware of the people around us, learning to see them through his eyes. Every person is important to God. You are important!

Stephens's life is a reminder. We don't know how long we have here on earth. God has designed this brief journey on earth to be an ongoing, interactive lesson of love that will ultimately bring us home. In the end, no matter what our situation, there will be nothing more important than who we have become and how we have touched the lives of others. Jesus' shed blood, his sacrifice, has made it possible for us to feed others with *true love*. We now have his presence, the Holy Spirit, to help us.

Don't waste this great sacrifice! Don't turn away from God's love; open up, embrace the gift of God's presence, and let his love pour through you to others. Set your course to finish well and hear the words of Jesus as we pass into eternal life, "Well done, good and faithful servant! ... Come and share your master's happiness!" (Matthew 25:21). We can then look forward to a new life after this one, as described in the book of Revelation.

> And I heard a loud voice from the throne saying, "Look! God's dwelling place is now among the people, and he will dwell with them. They will be his people, and God himself will be with them and be their God. 'He will wipe every tear from their eyes. There will be no more death' [the promise of Isaiah 25:8] or mourning or crying or pain, for the old order of things has passed away."
>
> He who was seated on the throne said, "I am making everything new!" Then he said, "Write this down, for these words are trustworthy and true."
>
> He said to me: "It is done. I am the Alpha and the Omega, the Beginning and the End. To the thirsty I will give water without cost from the spring of the water of life. Those who are victorious will inherit all this, and I will be their God and they will be my children." (Revelation 21:3–7)

No more death, crying, or pain, no more frustration! We will live in God's presence, surrounded by the beauty of nature and love. Imagine the amazing feeling of loving acceptance, far beyond anything we have ever experienced. We cannot fully grasp a life so beautiful, rich, and satisfying. Allow those around you to see a glimpse of this hope, this beautiful promise of what is to come, through your life. Set your heart, soul, mind, and strength on loving God and the people he created. Receive your destiny of light. Become a part of God's family tree—the love tree!

"You are the light of the world." (Matthew 5:14)

Those who are wise will shine like the brightness of the heavens, and those who lead many to righteousness, like the stars for ever and ever. (Daniel 12:3)

Then the King will say to those on his right, "Come you are blessed by my Father; take your inheritance, the kingdom prepared for you since the creation of the world. For I was hungry and you gave me something to eat, I was thirsty and you gave me something to drink, I was a stranger and you invited me in, I needed clothes and you clothed me, I was sick and you looked after me, was in prison and you came to visit me."

Then the righteous will answer him, "Lord, when did we see you hungry and feed you, or thirsty and give you something to drink? When did we see you a stranger and invite you in, or needing clothes and clothe you? When did we see you sick or in prison and go to visit you?"

The King will reply, "Truly I tell you, whatever you did for one of the least of these brothers and sisters of mine, you did for me." (Matthew 25:34–40)

For the LORD is good and his love endures forever;
    his faithfulness continues through all generations.
(Psalm 100:5)

Now to him who is able to do immeasurably more than all we ask or imagine, according to his power that is at work within us, to him be glory in the church and in Christ Jesus throughout all generations, for ever and ever! Amen. (Ephesians 3:20–21)

Now these three remain: faith, hope and love. But the greatest of these is love. (1 Corinthians 13:13)

Discussion:

1. What stage of life are you in? Are you content in that stage? Why or why not?
2. How does it help to keep an eternal perspective?
3. What has been most important to you as you look back on your life so far?
4. As you focus on the present, are there any changes you would like to make?
5. What steps could you take to experience more joy and fulfillment as you go forward?

ACKNOWLEDGMENTS

Family, friends, my church, and publisher all took part in bringing the story of *The Love Tree* to others.

Thank you to my sister, who encouraged me from beginning to end, believing in my ability to express God's love. Her hopeful words helped me keep working. She read through drafts and prayed for me along the way. I am grateful for her consistent and loving support.

Thanks to my children. My innovative and kind son, who makes the most of each day, just like his dad! His encouragement and pride in my writing accomplishments bring me joy. I thank my wise and lovely daughter, who worked on the first edits. Her invaluable suggestions created the structure. Thank you also for the valuable input of her husband. And my youngest—her loving nature and perseverance through tough times are inspiring. My children and grandchildren are leaves of love in our family tree!

I'd like to thank my aunt. When I was in treatment for cancer and too weak to carry on, though we live far apart, she was there for me with a calm voice and help with editing.

Thanks to many friends who willingly helped with editing, insight, and encouragement during this long journey. Thank you to my church—those who used the book as a group, and those who bought books to give to others after reading them. Thanks, Pastor, for your advice to highlight stories. I sincerely appreciate all of you.

Heartfelt thanks to my husband, who influenced my writing greatly, because it was through married life that I learned and grew the most. Without our life together, both the hard times and the good, I never could have written *The Love Tree*. After everything, he is the one who did a final edit before it went to the publisher's editorial staff. I value our relationship and look forward to our future.

Last but not least, I am so grateful to God, who has been my guide and absolute strength. He has taken me places and taught me lessons that I never expected. He has helped me express truths and remember passages, though my memory is not strong. I believe it was God's providence that led me to enroll in Bible College on an impulse, shortly before enrollment ended. I never thought that I would pursue that type of in-depth study. I never dreamed I would write a book. He has been my wind and my provider. God has blessed me abundantly, and I owe him my life!

Thankful,
Elyse Abiel

BIBLIOGRAPHY

Books

Batterson, Mark. *The Circle Maker: Praying Circles Around Your Biggest Dreams and Greatest Fears* (Grand Rapids: Zondervan, 2011).

Blackaby, Henry T., and Claude V. King. *Experiencing God, Knowing and Doing the will of God* (Nashville: Lifeway, 1990).

Tucker, Ruth Ann. *From Jerusalem to Irian Jaya* (Grand Rapids: Zondervan, 1983).

Holy Bible

Common English Bible (CEB). (Nashville: Common English Bible, 2011).

Good News Bible (GNB). (Philadelphia: American Bible Society, 1992).

New International Version (NIV). (Grand Rapids: Zondervan, 2011).

New International Version (NIV). (Colorado Springs: International Bible Society, 1984).

New Living Translation (NLT). (Carol Stream, Ill.: Tyndale House, 2007).

The Bible App

Reference

Vine's Complete Expository Dictionary (Nashville: Thomas Nelson, Inc., 1985).

Online Dictionaries:
   Dictionary app
   merriam-webster.com
   urbandictionary.com

Film

Ephron, Nora, dir. *Sleepless in Seattle*. 1993; Culver City, CA: TriStar Pictures.

Geronimi, Clyde, Wilfred Jackson, and Hamilton Luske, dirs. *Cinderella*. 1950; Los Angeles: Walt Disney Productions.

Websites

Feldman, Robert S. (2002) How often does the average person lie? Journal of Basic and Applied Psychology. Retrieved Dec. 4, 2012, from http://Curiosity.discovery.com (this website can no longer be found). Retrieved June 8, 2016, from https://www.umass.edu/newsoffice/article/umass-amherst-researcher -finds-most-people-lie-everyday-conversation.

Williams, Dr. Lisa. (2014) Why you should always say 'thank you': It's not just good manners – the two words helps [sic] maintain relationships, study claims. *Daily Mail, Science,* Article-2747790, Retrieved Oct. 2015 from http://www.dailymail.co.uk/sciencetech/article-2747790/Why-say-thank-It-s-not-just-good-manners-two-words-help-maintain-relationships-study-claims.html.

ABOUT THE AUTHOR

Elyse Abiel earned a bachelor's degree from Washington Bible College, receiving the Christian Service Award upon graduating in her late forties. As a young woman, Abiel worked in the design field and has an associate degree in mechanical design. She later owned a homemade ice cream shop to fund missions, teaming with her children and other teens. Family, worldwide travel, and volunteer work have all shaped her focus. Elyse has three children and five grandchildren.

CPSIA information can be obtained
at www.ICGtesting.com
Printed in the USA
BVHW041308041021
618099BV00012B/519